Folens History Book 2

Renaissance, Revolution and Reformation Britain 1485–1750

Aaron Wilkes

Editorial Consultant: Dean Smart

Author's acknowledgements

The author wishes to acknowledge Peter Burton and Nina Randall of Folens Publishers for their advice during the preparation of this book. He also wishes to thank his teaching colleague James Clayton for his practical suggestions and task preparation. He is particularly indebted to his wife, Emma, for the support she has given.

© 2003 Folens Limited, on behalf of the author.

United Kingdom: Folens Publishers, Apex Business Centre, Boscombe Road, Dunstable, LU5 4RL.

Email: folens@folens.com

Ireland: Folens Publishers, Greenhills Road, Tallaght, Dublin 24.

Email: info@folens.ie

Poland: JUKA, ul. Renesansowa 38, Warsaw 01-905.

Editor: Nina Randall

Series design, page layout and illustrations: Neil Sutton, Pumpkin House Cambridge

Picture researcher: Sue Sharp

Cover design: 2idesign Ltd., Cambridge

First published 2004 by Folens Limited.

Every effort has been made to trace the copyright holders of material used in this publication. If any copyright holder has been overlooked, we should be pleased to make any necessary arrangements.

British Library Cataloguing in Publication Data. A catalogue record for this publication is available from the British Library.

ISBN 1 84303 407 7

Acknowledgements

Bridgeman Art Library: 54 (second left), 55 (right) 70, 89, 91 (bottom); Bridgeman Art Library/ Bristol City Museum & Art Gallery: 23 (right); Bridgeman Art Library/ Gemaldegalerie, Berlin: 36 (top right); Bridgeman Art Library/ Kunsthistorisches Museum Vienna: 5, 21 (top left); Bridgeman Art Library/ Musee de Louvre: 21 (top right); Bridgeman Art Library/ Museum of Fine Arts Budapest: 106; Bridgeman Art Library/ Trustees of the Bedford Estate, Woburn Abbey: 31, 54 (middle); Bridgeman Art Library/ Wallace Collection: 98; British Library, Shelfmark/Man: Add.15760. F68v-69: 8; Corbis: 75; Corporation of London: 54 (left), 108; Fortean Picture Library: 119; Fotomas Index: 6, 7 (bottom), 23 (left), 29, 36 (bottom right), 63, 80, 81 (both), 86, 91 (top), 100, 103, 109, 110, 111; Shelfmark/Man: Add.42130.F172v Det: 36 (top left); Hulton Archive/ Mansell Collection: 84/85; Mary Evans Picture Library: 44, 57, 65, 66, 68, 69, 72, 95, 124 (both); Museum of English Rural Life: 118; National Maritime Museum: 36 (bottom left), 61; National Portrait Gallery: 13, 16, 20 (both), 28, 46, 55 (left); National Trust Photographic Library: 34, 35 (right), 35 (bottom); Neil Setchfield: 107; Public Record Office: 99; Richard Tillbrook/ Norfolk County Council Library: 93; Royal Collection Enterprises Limited © HM Queen Elizabeth II: 21 (bottom), 27, 32, 53, 116 (left); Scottish National Portrait Gallery: 123; Scottish Viewpoint Picture Library: 35 (top left).

'Book of Martyrs', John Fox, Ambassador Productions Ltd, 1995: 29; 'Crown and Country, Britain 1500-1750, Homework and Extension Pack', Martyn Wiltcock and John D. Clare, Hodder, 2000: 94, 95; 'History Alive 1 1485-1714', Peter Moss, Hart-Davis Education Ltd., 1980: 28, 85, 94, 95, 107; 'In Search of History 1485-1714', J.F. Aylett, Hodder Arnold, 1984: 107; 'Oliver Cromwell and His World', Maurice Ashley, Thames & Hudson, 1972: 85; 'Past into Present 2, 1400-1700', Mary Carter, Christopher Culpin and Nicholas Kinloch, Collins Educational, 1990: 87; Quest: 'The World of Enlightenment', Bea Stimpson, Nelson Thornes, 1999: 95; Quest: 'The World of Enlightenment, Activity Support Guide', Simon Rodden, Norman Hobson and Bea Stimpson, Nelson Thornes, 1999: 83, 112; SHP 'Discovering the Making of the UK', John Murray, published by Colin Shephard and Tim Lomas, 1995: 81, 87, 88, 94; SHP 'Medicine and Health through Time', Ian Dawson and Ian Coulson, John Murray Publications Ltd., 1996: 112; 'The Mary Rose', Mary Rose Trust, 1981: 25.

Contents

Introduction

Britain in 1485

 AIMS

▶ What was Britain like in 1485?
▶ What relationship did England have with her immediate neighbours?

This book is about the people and events of Britain between 1485 and 1750, a time of great change. For you to see how important these changes were, you must first find out about Britain in 1485. Then, towards the end of this book, you will be asked to compare the Britain of 1485 with the Britain of 1750.

A Lord

I am Henry VII, King of England. I rule other countries too. I won my crown on the battlefield and I intend to keep it. There are many rich and powerful men in this country, so I must work hard to control them.

Henry VII

We lords are rich and powerful... and the King knows it! We own lots of land and sometimes help the King to make decisions. If all lords joined together we could be strong enough to defeat the King.

England and Scotland are separate countries. The English and the Scots have fought a lot over the years. I think of the English as the 'old enemy' and truly hate them! There are about half a million Scots.

A Scotsman

Like most of the **population**, we are poor and live in the countryside. Some of the land is used for growing crops or grazing sheep, but most is woodland or wasteland. We live on what we grow. If we grow more than we need, we sell it at the local market in the nearest town. Most towns are still quite small, but a few are growing fast. Only 10% of people live in the towns. There are about two million people who live in England now.

Over the years, English kings have tried to control us but have failed. They have only managed to control a small part of this country. About 800 000 people live here.

An Irish Chief

A Welsh Prince

The English control most of Wales but some areas are still run by **independent** Welsh princes like me. There are only about 200 000 people in Wales.

There is only one religion... Christianity. The Head of the Church is the Pope who lives in Rome. Religion is a very important part of people's lives.

A Priest

A Villager

KEY

English land ruled by English King

Irish land ruled by English lords with English laws

Irish land ruled mostly by the English King, with Irish laws

Welsh land ruled mostly by the English King, with Welsh laws

Welsh land ruled by English Prince of Wales, with English laws

Scotland – an independent country from England

SCOTLAND

IRELAND

WALES

ENGLAND

Wales had been conquered by England.

England was ruled by a king – Henry VII.

Calais – the only part of France still ruled by England.

Source A ◄ Britain in 1485

HUNGRY FOR MORE?

What was your town like in 1485? Can you find out anything about it? Try your local library, the Internet or ask your teacher.

! WISE UP WORDS

independent   population

Source B ▼ People enjoying themselves in 1485

WORK

1 Write out this paragraph, choosing one answer from each pair of brackets.
In 1485, the King of England was (Henry VII/Henry VIII). He also controlled most of (Wales/Scotland) and part of Ireland. (Wales/Scotland) was an independent country. Some land was used for (fishing/farming) but most of it was wasteland or (woodland/Disneyland). Nine out of (ten/nine) people lived in the (towns/countryside) and grew enough food to live on. If they grew (more/less) than they needed, they might go and sell it at the local (supermarket/market).

2 a Draw a bar chart to show the population of England, Scotland, Ireland and Wales in 1485. Your teacher will help you to set this out properly. Make sure you add a title.

 b Find out the population of England, Scotland, Ireland and Wales today. Draw another bar chart using these figures. Underneath it write a paragraph comparing the two bar charts.
    – Does England still have the largest population?
    – What is the second most populated country?

3 Look at **Source B**. People would have enjoyed themselves like this in 1485. With a partner, list as many games and activities as you can. You should be able to spot at least 8, including the boy tied up in a knot!

4 Divide a page into two columns. Write 'Britain in 1485' at the top of one column and 'Britain now' at the top of the other. List all the ways that Britain in 1485 was different from Britain today. Choose what you think are the three most important differences and write a sentence or two explaining why you made your choices.

The man who wanted to know everything

▶ Who was Leonardo da Vinci and why is he such an important figure?
▶ What was the 'Renaissance'?

During the Middle Ages, all books had to be written out by hand. This took a long time so books were both rare and expensive. The work was done by monks so most of the books were bibles, prayer books or religious stories.

After the invention of the **printing press** in about 1450, more and more books were printed, rather than copied out. Printing was still a slow process, but it was faster than the handwritten work of monks. As more books were published, more people wanted to read. It became fashionable to write books as well as read them. Soon there were books on fishing, hunting, chess, medicine, travel and different religions.

Source A ▲ A printer's shop, 1520

Scholars soon began to read the old books written by the Greeks and Romans who lived before Christ. They found, to their amazement, that the Greeks and Romans knew a lot more than people had realised. Across Europe, writers, sculptors, doctors, mathematicians, scientists and architects started to realise that some of their current ideas were wrong and there were often better ways of doing some things. They began to ask questions and experiment with new ideas. For years, people had accepted that the Bible had all the answers to their questions. Now educated people wanted to find out things for themselves.

One man who was fascinated by these ideas was Leonardo da Vinci, who had been born in Italy in 1452. He was a painter, scientist, engineer, musician and poet. He has been called 'the man who wanted to know everything'.

Leonardo the genius

Leonardo da Vinci was a **genius** who was desperate to be the best at everything he did. Through his experiments he worked out how the human eye worked and was the first to study a human **embryo** in detail. He studied fossils, oil painting – can you name his most famous painting? – glass making and weapon building. Every day he made a list of things to do!

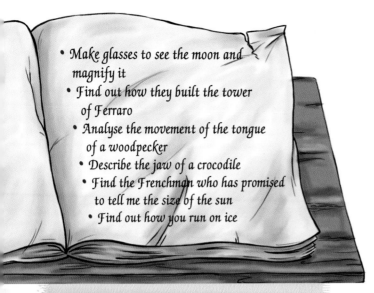

- Make glasses to see the moon and magnify it
- Find out how they built the tower of Ferraro
- Analyse the movement of the tongue of a woodpecker
- Describe the jaw of a crocodile
- Find the Frenchman who has promised to tell me the size of the sun
- Find out how you run on ice

Source B ▲ This list is copied from Leonardo's original Italian notes

Many of his ideas concerned war and flying. He dreamed of building some of the finest weapons the world had ever seen and of designing a machine that would allow man to fly like a bird. He also designed helicopters, canals, cranes, a snorkel, a lifebelt and a submarine. He even made an alarm clock that tipped water onto a sleeping person to wake them up! Some of his sketched ideas for inventions clearly show that he thought of doing things hundreds of years before anyone else.

Source C ▲ Leonardo's tank, made from wood and steel with a cannon in the 'tortoise shell' roof. The first tanks were not used in war until 1916.

Leonardo was not alone in his fascination with learning about the world. Over the years, many men would make fascinating discoveries in the worlds of science, medicine and engineering. This period of discovery is known as the '**Renaissance**', an Italian word meaning 'reborn'. To many, it seemed as if their new knowledge and ideas were allowing them to see the world clearly for the first time ever. They really felt that they had been 'reborn'.

PAUSE FOR THOUGHT

Leonardo was very secretive about some of his ideas and when describing them in his notes, he wrote backwards, from right to left, so they could only be read in a mirror. Why do you think that he wanted some of his ideas kept a secret?

! WISE UP WORDS

Renaissance   printing press   genius   embryo

WORK

1 Copy and complete the following sentences:
  a Leonardo da Vinci was born in _____ in 1452.
  b Many people consider Leonardo to be a _____.
  c Many of his ideas are concerned with _____ and _____.
  d In order to keep his ideas secret he would often write _____.
  e Leonardo would make a _____ of new things to find out every day.

2 Why and how did the invention of the printing press lead to a greater learning in Europe?

3 Look at **Source B**. What does this list tell you about the sort of man Leonardo was?

4 Why is this period of history often referred to as the 'Renaissance'?

5 Be like Leonardo! Design your own alarm clock that tips water on your head to wake you. Remember, no electricity!

The world: is it flat or round?

▸ What theories existed in 1485 regarding the shape of the world?
▸ Why did explorers want to sail to other continents?

In 1485, when Henry VII became King of England, most people thought the world was shaped like a plate. They believed it was quite flat with most of the land near the centre and water all around the edge. If a ship sailed too near the edge, it might fall off!

The true size and shape of the earth wasn't really understood. Europeans obviously knew about European lands such as England, France, Spain and Italy. They also knew of the Holy Land (then ruled by Turks), northern Africa and the Eastern lands such as China and India. Other than that, they weren't sure! For years, most people brave enough to successfully travel overland to the East to trade had made a fortune. They brought back precious **spices**, silks, perfumes and jewels from India and China. These could be sold for huge profits.

However, the dangerous journey overland and back could take over three years – and the Turks charged traders a fortune to pass through their lands.

Source A ▾ Map of the world drawn by Henricus Martellus in 1489

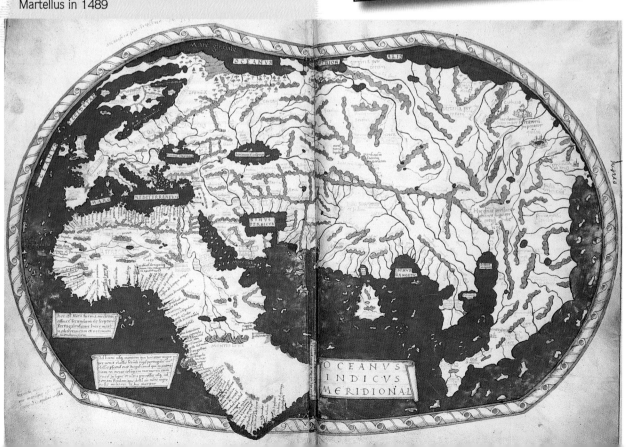

LADIES

Fed up with wool and linen?

Always dressed in the same fabrics as your neighbour?

Buy Eastern silk instead

A silk gown will put you in a class above the rest

BUY IT HERE

was ball shaped. This theory was based on a book called Geography, written by a Greek writer called Ptolemy in about AD100. People started to reread it in the 1400s.

Several brave explorers, excited by the stories of adventure in Marco Polo's book, decided to try and venture further than man had ever sailed before. One man, Christopher Columbus, even thought it might be possible to sail west across the Atlantic Ocean in order to reach the East. In other words, go all around the ball-shaped earth by sea, instead of having to go overland. Remember, he had absolutely no idea that the **continent** of America was there! Some people thought he was mad; Columbus just hoped that it would make him rich.

PAUSE FOR THOUGHT

Why do you think that people thought the world was flat? Also, why do you think that they thought it was possible to fall off the edge? Clue: Horizon

In 1477, the adventures of a famous **explorer** from the Middle Ages, Marco Polo, were published. Other explorers began to read them. Around this time there was a growing belief that the world wasn't flat at all but

Source B ▾ Written by Columbus in 1492

'Oh most excellent gold! Whoever has gold has treasure, which gives him the power to do what he wants. It lets him do what he wants in the world and even helps souls to heaven.'

WISE UP WORDS

spices   continent   explorer

WORK

1 Copy and complete the following paragraph. Use the ten words in the word box below:

In early Tudor times, most people thought that the world was _____. They thought that if a _____ sailed too close to the _____, it might fall off. Christopher _____ was an _____ who thought that the world was shaped like a _____. He thought it was possible to sail _____ across the _____ Ocean in order to reach the Spice Islands and _____ in the _____.

> East   flat   Columbus   edge   ball   west
> explorer   Atlantic   India   ship

2 Look at **Source A**.

   a How can you tell that a lot was known about the west coast of Africa in 1489, but not the east coast?

   b Make a list of some of the places Europeans had not discovered in 1489. You might need to look in a modern atlas.

3 Why were some European traders and explorers keen to find a new route to the East and explore new land?

4 Write about the parts played by the following in encouraging explorers to look for new lands:

   a Marco Polo

   b Ptolemy

5 Imagine you are a Tudor trader who has just arrived back in England or Wales with a selection of goods from the East. Design a sales poster to advertise your spices, silks and perfumes. Use some of the adverts on these pages to inspire you. You might want to mention how difficult the journey was to get these products home.

They all laughed at Christopher Columbus

AIMS
▸ How did Christopher Columbus discover the 'New World'?
▸ What new goods came from the 'New World'?

Christopher Columbus had a theory. He thought that it was possible to reach China and India by sailing west, rather than having to travel east across dangerous lands. He was convinced that he could sail right around the globe and arrive in the East by sea.

Columbus first tried to borrow money for his journey from the kings of England, Portugal and France. They all refused. Eventually, tempted by the promise of gold and spices, Queen Isabella of Spain funded his voyage.

He then bought three ships, the Pinta, the Nina and the Santa Maria and hired 100 men to act as his crew. He set off on 3 August 1492.

The **voyage** went well for about six weeks. The crew occasionally went swimming, fished and sang together. Columbus read passages from the Bible to the men. However, by early October the crew were becoming unhappy. Water and food supplies were getting low and there was no sign of India or China. Was Columbus wrong? Perhaps the world wasn't a **sphere** after all? Were they about to fall off the edge of the world?

On 12 October, Columbus' luck changed when a lookout on the Pinta spotted land. Columbus went

ashore and named the island San Salvador, meaning 'Holy Saviour' (it is now known as Watling Island). He spent the next few months sailing around the islands of Cuba and Haiti. He found **natives** of these islands and kidnapped six of them to take back to Queen Isabella! He also took some gold, several fish and a parrot.

Columbus returned home to a hero's welcome. He made three more trips to these new islands and on one journey, landed on the South American mainland. Until his death in 1506, Columbus still thought he'd found a new route to India or China. In fact, we still call the islands he visited the 'West Indies'. Columbus had no idea that he had found a continent, America, which Europeans did not know existed. Only in later years after explorers had found other lands, did people realise that Columbus had discovered a 'New World'.

FACT: ▸ 'I saw it first … no I saw it first'

▸ The lookout on the Pinta who first spotted land was called Rodrigo. As Queen Isabella had offered a reward for the first man to sight land, Rodrigo thought he was about to receive a pension, every year for life. However, Columbus kept the money for himself... he argued that it was his voyage, so it should be his reward.

Source A ▾ From the logbook of Columbus' ships

10 October 1492

'He navigated west-south-west. They went ten miles an hour and at times twelve and sometimes seven. The men could now bear no more. They complained of the long voyage. But Admiral Columbus cheered them as best he could, holding out bright hopes of the gains they could make. He said God would keep them safe.'

Columbus – the first of many

Columbus' success inspired other explorers. The promise of wealth, better maps, compasses and sails meant that more people would travel the world.

- Vasco de Gama (from Portugal) – In 1498, he proved it was possible to reach India by sailing around the bottom of Africa and up the eastern coast.
- Amerigo Vespucci (from Spain) – From 1499 to 1503, he continued exploring the area where Columbus had sailed. Some people think America was named after him.
- Ferdinand Magellan (from Portugal) – On 20 September 1519, five ships and 234 men set off on a journey around the world. Magellan, the leader, died on the voyage but his crew sailed on. One ship and 18 men made it home in 1522.
- John Cabot (from England) – In 1497, he tried to reach Asia by sailing north-west. He sailed to Canada.

FACT: ▶ New goods

Explorers brought back interesting new goods from their voyages. These items had never been seen in Europe before… and were a huge success. They included tomatoes, tobacco, potatoes, turkeys and cocoa.

Source B ▼ A modern map showing the routes taken by explorers, 1492–1498

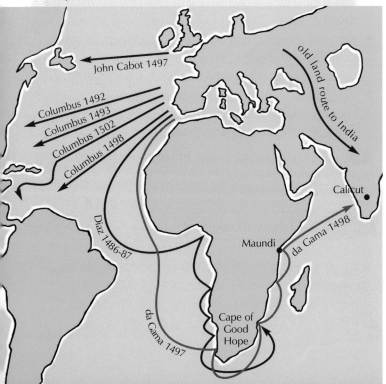

! WISE UP WORDS

voyage   sphere   natives

Summary

- By the end of the Middle Ages, more and more people were starting to think that the world was a sphere and not flat.
- By the beginning of the 1500s, Europeans were exploring distant lands and discovering what they described as 'New Worlds'.
- There was a lot of trade between Europe, the Holy Land, India and China. The discovering of 'New Worlds' brought new goods, such as tobacco, tomatoes and cocoa into Europe.
- There was trade with Africa as well, especially between Spain, Portugal and Mediterranean countries.

WORK

1 True or False?

Write the following sentences into your books. Next to each sentence, write if it is true or false. If you believe a sentence is false, rewrite the corrected sentence underneath.

- Vasco de Gama reached India by sailing around the bottom of Italy.
- America is named after the British explorer Amerigo Vespucci.
- Ferdinand Magellan did not survive the first full journey around the world.
- John Cabot, from Scotland, discovered Australia.

2 Read **Source A** carefully.

a What examples can you give to show Columbus was a strong leader?

b Make up your own logbook entry for 12 October. Remember to mention Rodrigo.

3 a Where did Columbus think he had discovered in 1492?

b Was he correct?

4 Explorers were treated as heroes at this time – why do you think this was?

5 Imagine you are a ship's captain returning with 'new' goods from distant lands. Write a letter to a friend describing some of these new goods. (Good luck describing a turkey!)

11

Was King Henry VII a gangster?

 AIMS
▶ How did the first Tudor King deal with the problems of England and Wales?
▶ What tactics did Henry VII use to become more powerful?

PAUSE **FOR** **THOUGHT**

> *Have you heard of the word 'gangster'? Some of you will have, but what is a gangster? Talk about what the word means.*

A **gangster** is usually a very powerful criminal. They squeeze money out of people and they make deals to make themselves more powerful. They often live fantastically lavish lives and enjoy showing off their wealth and power. They also have weapons with which to bully people. Henry VII was not a criminal; he was King of England and Wales. But now you know what a gangster is, see if you think Henry VII acted like one...

For 30 years, in the fifteenth century, the York family and the Lancaster family had been fighting for control England. By 1485, it was the Yorks who ruled the lan The most senior Yorkist, Richard, had been crowned King Richard III of England in 1483.

In August 1485, a member of the Lancaster family, Henry Tudor, decided to try to win the crown for his family. On 22 August, in a field near Bosworth, Leicestershire, the two armies fought each other.

King Richard decided to wear his crown into battle but this made him very easy to spot. As he charged towards his enemy, he was pulled from his horse by some of Henry's bodyguards. They cut Richard to pieces. Legend has it that they found Richard's bloodstained crown in a thorn bush before placing it on Henry Tudor's head. He became King Henry VII, the first Tudor king.

The new King had won his crown by fighting. Now he had the job of keeping it.

The new King had major problems:
- The York family would probably seek revenge for the death of Richard III. Could he buy them off instead?
- Some of the country's landowning barons were very powerful and wealthy. They also kept their own private armies. How could he reduce their power?
- Kings need money for weapons, armies, large country houses and entertainment. Henry didn't have much. How could he get rich quick?

As you will see, King Henry would need to use every gangster trick in the book.

FACT: ▶ Cheeky monkey

▶ Henry VII owned a pet monkey, which used to cause mayhem in his palaces. It once managed to open a box in which the King kept all his diaries... and ate them.

Source A ▾ Painting of Henry VII dating from 1505. Notice he is clutching a rose in his right hand, one of the many Tudor symbols. We still use the rose today as an English symbol. Can you think where it is used?

Anno 1505 29 octobz imago henzich vii tzaurg zege illuzzllmi

WORK

1 What is meant by the term 'gangster'?

2 Imagine you are Henry VII and have just been crowned King of England. Write a letter to one of your friends outlining your concerns as the new King. Think about the problems he faced as the new King.

So how did Henry solve his problems?

① **He married a woman from the House of York.**

Henry settled the old argument between the Lancasters and the Yorks. In early 1486, he married Elizabeth of York, daughter of Edward VI. Now the Lancasters had a king and the Yorks had a queen.

The white rose symbol of the Yorks was added to the red rose symbol of the Lancaster family to make the Tudor Rose.

② **He banned private armies.**

Some barons paid their servants to act as an army for them. Henry banned this. He was worried a baron could use his own private army against the King. Henry once visited his friend, the Earl of Oxford, who had lined up his servants in uniform along his drive to welcome the King. Henry took a few moments to admire the beautiful uniforms... and then fined the earl £10 000 for keeping a private army!

③ **Henry made sure that he had the best cannons.**

The cannon and gunpowder were changing warfare at this time. With some of the finest cannons in the land, Henry made the Barons' castles unsafe.

⑤ **He made deals with other countries.**

Henry had to raise taxes to pay for war with France, but then he managed to get the French King to pay him £150 000 not to fight. To make sure that England didn't get involved in a costly war with Spain, he got his eldest son, Arthur, married to a Spanish princess, Catherine of Aragon. When Arthur died, Henry got his younger son, also called Henry, married to her as well. He also got his daughter to marry the son of the King of Scotland.

⑥ **He made sure everyone knew he was King.**

Henry wanted to be seen as a great king. He used family **symbols** to show people the strength of the Tudors. They appeared all over England in churches, cathedrals, palaces and manor houses.

The Tudor Rose

The Beaufort Portcullis, the symbol of his mother Margaret.

Crown and thorn bush. Why do you think this symbol was used?

French lilies. Henry had spent a lot of time in France.

Henry spent a fortune on entertainment, lavish banquets, processions, tournaments, dancing and music. He once paid £30.00 (a fortune) to a girl who danced for him. He even made his dogs wear fancy silk costumes! Even so, by the time of his death in 1509, Henry VII had left his surviving son, Henry, a fortune. England was at peace and his throne was safe.

4 He forced people to give him money.

Henry sent his ministers around England looking for sources of income. If they found a large manor house, they would force the owner to give them money. The ministers would argue that the house was so nice, the owner obviously had enough money to lend some to the King. Alternatively, if they came across a smaller house that was in need of repair, the ministers would still demand money. They would argue that the owner was obviously saving his money rather than spending it, and so must have enough savings to give some money to the King. The lenders would never get their money back.

Source B ▾ Some payments made by Henry between 1492 and 1494, taken from court records

1492

8 Jan: For the King to play at cards £5.00
16 Jan: For one who brought the King a lion £2.66½
29 Jan: To Lady York for minstrels £1.00
12 Feb: For a fool who entertained 33p
29 April: For a flute player 33p
4 Jun: For the King's loss at gambling with his crossbow . 66p
10 Jun: For a Spanish man who played the fool £2.00
30 Jun: For the King, which he lost at cards £40.00
31 Jul: For a horse and saddle to give to the Spanish fool . 92½p
1 Aug: For children who sang in the garden 16½p

1493

23 Jun: For making a bonfire on Midsummer Eve 50p
25 Aug: For a young girl who danced £30.00
24 Sept: For a man who had his bull baited 50p

1494

13 Jun: For a Spanish tennis player £2.00
14 Aug: For the King's loss at tennis £1.38

WISE UP WORDS

symbols   gangster

WORK

1 Read **Source B**.

a Name five different amusements that Henry enjoyed.

b Look carefully. What evidence is there, other than the £2.00 paid to him, that Henry enjoyed watching the Spanish fool?

2 Again, imagine you are Henry VII and you have been on the throne a number of years. Write back to your friend and tell them how you have dealt with the problems that faced you.

– Have you made friends with the York family? If so, how?
– Do you feel secure from enemies, both inside England and abroad?
– Are you rich? If so, how did you make your money? What sort of lifestyle do you lead?

3 Look back at your definition of a 'gangster'. Was Henry VII like a gangster?

What was young Henry VIII like?

AIMS
▶ How did young King Henry VIII spend his time… and money?
▶ Was he a religious man?

Everybody has heard of Henry VIII. Most people think they know a few things about him too. They usually say:

- He was a big fat bloke.

- He had six wives… or was it eight?

- He beheaded most of his wives!

Some of these statements are true. Henry did have six wives, but he didn't chop the heads off most of them, although he did get someone to behead two! As for him being a big fat bloke – well yes he was – but only for the last few years of his life. In fact, on his forty-fifth birthday, Henry was the same size as he was when he was 23 – and at that age, Henry was a fine sportsman. As a young man, he enjoyed hunting, tennis, wrestling, archery and jousting. He was even known to enjoy a good snowball fight in winter. Henry wrote music and poetry and could speak four languages. So despite having a bit of a weight problem when he was older, Henry was an impressive man when he was crowned in 1509.

As you will learn, many fantastic facts surround the life of Henry VIII. In fact, Henry was desperate to become known as a super king and even liked to call himself 'Henry the Great'. But although he is most famous for his wives, the most important events in Henry's life were the religious changes he made. Not only did they affect religion in Henry's time, they changed religion in England and Wales for good.

Source A ◀ A portrait of Henry VIII showing him in his late twenties

Henry was a very religious man and, like most people in the country at the time, he was **Catholic**. He visited church at least three times a day and even wrote a book supporting the **Pope**, who was the Head of the Catholic Church. Henry was such a good Catholic that in 1521, the Pope rewarded Henry with the title 'Fidei Defensor', which means 'Defender of the Faith'. Henry liked the title so much that he made sure the letters FD were on all the coins made in his name. You can still see the letters FD or the words Fid. Def. on some British coins today – have a look yourself.

However, by 1533, Henry had fallen out with the Pope who **excommunicated** him, meaning he was expelled from the Catholic Church. This was a very serious punishment at the time because it meant that the person could not talk to a priest about their sins. If a priest did not forgive you for your sins, then you wouldn't get to heaven. So how did Henry VIII and the Pope fall out with each other? What had Henry done that was so terrible that he received the worst kind of religious punishment? The next few pages chart an amazing story.

FACT: ▶ Henry, the good Catholic

▸ Henry's book said how good the Catholic Church was. In it he wrote that the Pope, as Head of the Catholic Church, did a good job. Henry even wrote about marriage, which he said should be forever – one woman, for life.

Henry the big spender

Henry loved to bet on anything – cards, dice, tennis, wrestling, or jousting. He used to win (and lose) the equivalent of thousands of pounds every day. Henry also loved to dress in the smartest, most expensive clothes. His silk shirts, gold buttons and jewel-encrusted jackets would have cost a fortune. So too would his legendary parties, held at any of Henry's 55 palaces.

FACT: ▶ What a job!

▸ Henry VIII employed someone to wipe his bottom! He was officially called the 'Groom of the Stool'. It was a much prized job because the employee got to spend so much time with the King!

TONIGHT ONLY

AT HAMPTON COURT PALACE IN THE PRESENCE OF HENRY THE GREAT

A ROYAL GALA PERFORMANCE

A feast fit for a king – beef, pork, lamb, chicken, eggs, venison, pigeon pie, rabbit, wine and apple tart

Anne Penn – plays the harp

Fat Scotty the jester – jokes and rude stories

Matthew Morrish – the little juggling stilt walker

The fighting Dunkley Brothers – will wrestle each other and any challengers – Prizes to be won

Dance the Pavane, the Volta and the Galliard to the wonderful music makers followed by – STOP PRESS – Hear our King's latest song 'GREENSLEEVES'

WISE UP WORDS

excommunicated   Catholic   Pope

WORK

Your task is to write a profile of the young King Henry VIII.

Search through the text to find out details about the young King, using the following subheadings to guide your writing:

- Henry the athlete
- Henry the good Catholic
- Henry the big spender

Finally, write your own opinion in answer to the following question – Should the young King Henry have been called 'Henry the Great'?

Henry VIII, his first wife and his big problem...

▶ Why did Henry VIII fall out with the Pope?
▶ How did England change as a result?

The problems Henry had with the Pope originated in Henry's love life. His first wife was a Spanish princess called Catherine of Aragon. He first met her in 1501 when she was sent to England to marry Arthur, Henry's older brother. Everyone expected Arthur would be King of England when his father Henry VII died.

A marriage between Prince Arthur and Princess Catherine would mean friendship between England and Spain. However, Arthur died only a year after the marriage. To avoid sending widow Catherine home to Spain and upsetting her father, Henry VII arranged for his second son, Henry, to marry her. The wedding took place in 1509, the same year that the old King Henry VII died. Seventeen-year-old Henry became King Henry VIII and Catherine of Aragon was his first queen.

Henry and Catherine were a popular and loving couple. In 1513, whilst Henry was in France, Catherine ran the country for him. Her army even beat a Scottish army at the Battle of Flodden. Catherine brought Henry a present home from the battle... the dead King of Scotland's coat, still stained with his blood.

Henry and Catherine were happily married for nearly 20 years. Henry once said, 'If I were still free, I would choose her for a wife above all others.' What a romantic man! But the marriage didn't last. As we all know, he had five more wive after Catherine... so what went wrong?

Present for you darling...

Cheers dear...

Henry desperately wanted a son.

It's a girl!

Catherine gives birth to six children, but only one, a girl called Mary, survives.

By 1527, Henry thinks Catherine is too old to have any more children.

Henry wants to divorce Catherine. He'd fallen in love with another woman too - Anne Boleyn!

Henry gets his lawyers to secretly look into whether his marriage to Catherine is legal or not.

The marriage was found to be legal - but Henry still wanted his divorce.

Henry's only chance of a divorce was to ask the Pope. He was the only man who could give Henry his divorce.

Henry hated the fact that the Pope had this power over him... but he had a plan.

Henry ignored the Pope. He made himself Head of the Church of England instead of the Pope.

The Pope was furious but Henry could do as he pleased.

In 1533, Henry gave himself the divorce he desired.

Henry could now marry Anne Boleyn.

Henry married his second wife, Anne Boleyn, in the summer of 1533. She was already pregnant.

It's another girl!

Anne gave birth to a girl, Elizabeth, in September 1533. Henry was very disappointed – why?

Some of the monks in England didn't support Henry's new Church of England. They supported the Pope.

So he closed down all the monasteries and the land was sold.

The monasteries were very wealthy and the King made a good profit.

But the Pope was furious again. Not only had Henry ignored him and closed all of the Catholic monasteries in England, but he had now stolen all their treasures.

WISE UP WORDS

Reformation   Dissolution

Henry's desire for a baby boy began a series of events that altered religion in England forever. In one move, he had his divorce and made himself more powerful. The Pope in Rome no longer had the English Church under his control – Henry did and all its wealth too! To this day, the Head of the Church of England is the king or queen. Yet despite this change of church leader and the closing of the monasteries, Henry only really made one other major religious change. From 1538, he ordered that in every church the Bible was to be read in English, not Latin. At last, ordinary people could understand what their religion was teaching them.

FACT: ▶ New titles for new things

▶ Historians like to give titles to anything different! Henry's changes to the Church are known as the '**Reformation**' because Henry was reforming (another word for 'changing') the English Church.

When he closed down the monasteries, it was known as the '**Dissolution**' of the monasteries. Dissolution is another word for 'breaking up'.

WORK

1 The following dates are important ones from Henry's marriage to his first wife:

   1533 • 1527 • 1513 • 1501 • 1509

   Write each date in chronological order on a separate line. Beside each date, write what happened in each year. Be careful – LOTS happens in one of the years!

2 What do we see as unusual today about Henry's marriage to Catherine of Aragon?

3 Which of the following statements do you think was most important in making Henry want a divorce from Catherine of Aragon?
   • Henry was bored with Catherine
   • Henry's desire to have a son
   • Henry's love of Anne Boleyn
   Give reasons for your answer.

4 a Why did Henry want a son?
   b What do you think about his reason?

5 Why did Henry close down the monasteries? Give more than one reason.

6 Write a sentence or two to explain the following words:
   Reformation • Dissolution

Who'd want to be married to Henry VIII?

▸ Why did Henry marry so many women?
▸ What happened to each of them?

Henry VIII had more wives than any other English or Welsh king. Being his wife must have been a tricky business. You might have enjoyed the luxury lifestyle for a time, but there were certain risks involved in being married to a man like Henry.

- He accused one wife of being a witch.
- He divorced another for being too ugly.
- He sentenced another to death for having a boyfriend before she met the King!

Your task is to look through the tangled love life of Henry. Imagine that you are a friend of Catherine Parr. She is a sensible, intelligent and kind 31-year-old widow and 52-year-old King Henry wants to marry her. She would be Henry's sixth wife. Despite her family's pleasure that the King has chosen her, she is a little bit worried, perhaps frightened. The marriage has been organised and the date set for 12 July 1543. Your job as her friend is to give her advice. Carefully read about each of Henry's previous wives and what went wrong for each of them. Catherine is looking to you for guidance. How might she be able to keep the King happy? What shouldn't she do?

Let's start by looking at the ageing King...
- 52 years old.
- Cruel, bad tempered and paranoid – once he was so convinced that someone would try to kill him as he slept that he instructed a bricklayer to brick him into his bedroom at night.
- So fat that he had to be put onto his horse with a hoist.
- He complained about headaches, fever, smallpox and malaria. His legs were covered with ulcers, which later turned to gangrene. One visitor wrote that Henry 'had the worst legs in the world'.

Catherine of Aragon: Wife Number 1: 1509–33

- A Spanish princess, once married to Henry's older brother. She brought friendship with Spain.
- Clever and popular.
- All her male babies died but she had a daughter called Mary who survived.
- Henry thought Catherine was old and boring when she reached 40 years of age. He divorced her.

? DID YOU KNOW?

Henry had a party to celebrate Catherine's death in 1536 (there were rumours at the time that she'd been poisoned). He even wore yellow clothes, the traditional colour of celebration!

Anne Boleyn: Wife Number 2: 1533–36

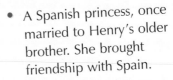

- Young, sexy and very fashionable.
- Made Henry wait for sex until he married her.
- Had a daughter, Elizabeth. Henry sulked for weeks because he wanted a boy.
- Miscarried a baby boy in 1536.
- Henry accused Anne of having sex with four men and her brother (yes, her brother). Despite no proof, she was beheaded in 1536.

? DID YOU KNOW?

Anne was born with an extra finger on one hand. People said that this was a sign that she was a witch. Anne made enemies easily.

Jane Seymour: Wife Number 3: 1536–37

- Calm, gentle and caring. She tried hard to be friends with Henry's daughters.
- Made Henry wait for sex until he married her.
- Had a son, Edward Henry was delighted – a boy at last!
- Jane died of an infection a few days after the birth.

? DID YOU KNOW?

Henry really loved Jane. More than two years went by before he married again, the longest gap between his marriages. When he died, he was buried next to her.

Catherine Howard: Wife Number 5: 1540–42

- Young, lively and very pretty.
- She flirted with lots of men… and Henry found out. She once finished off a letter to her lover with the words, 'Yours as long as life endures'. Henry was furious.
- Henry also found out that she had several serious boyfriends before she met the King. A queen should not have a past like this!
- She was executed.

? DID YOU KNOW?

When Catherine found out she was going to be beheaded, she ran shouting and screaming towards Henry to beg his forgiveness. He locked the door and ignored her. Her crying ghost is still said to haunt the same corridor at Hampton Court Palace.

Anne of Cleves: Wife Number 4: 1540

- Cleves was an area of what is now Germany, close to Flanders and France. Henry married Anne because it brought friendship between England, Wales and this powerful European region.
- She was serious and unfashionable. Friends tried to teach her some of Henry's favourite card games but she didn't understand them.
- Henry had seen a painting of her and liked what he saw. However, when he saw her for real, he described her as a 'fat mare [horse] from Flanders'.
- Henry divorced her.

? DID YOU KNOW?

Their six-month marriage was never consummated (they never had sex). After the divorce, Anne was given land, money and the rather strange official title of the 'King's sister'.

WORK

Now write Catherine a letter giving her advice about her forthcoming marriage. In your letter include:

– Details of his previous five marriages
  - What attracted Henry to each of them?
  - What went wrong with each marriage?
  - What happened to each of them?

– Top tips on how to keep Henry happy and interested in her. Remember how old he is and what sort of wife he needs now.

HUNGRY FOR MORE? *What happened to Catherine Parr? Find out about her life with Henry… and after.*

A changing Church

AIMS
▸ Why did some people criticise the Catholic Church?
▸ Who were the Protestants?

How many of you have been to a church or other place of worship in the last few days… or weeks… or months?
Who has prayed recently, chatted to the local vicar or religious leader, or been on a journey to the nearest cathedral?

For some people today, it is very difficult to imagine the importance of the Church in everyone's lives years ago. Today, lots of people only visit a church for weddings, christenings or funerals. It was very different in Tudor times. There were no televisions, cinemas or shopping centres. There weren't too many books or organised sports matches either. Houses weren't full of carpets, comfy chairs and sofa beds. However, there was the local church – a welcoming meeting place, a place to enjoy summer fairs, have a chat with friends and, of course, to worship God.

Spreading the word

In Tudor times, everyone believed in God. They used God to explain things they didn't understand. Nasty illnesses or infections were seen as punishment from God. If the harvest was bad, it was because God wished it so. They also believed that heaven and hell were real places. If you led a good life on earth and prayed regularly, then you would probably go to heaven when you died. However, if you were a bad person who committed crimes and didn't attend church regularly, then you would definitely end up in hell.

By 1500, there were thousands of books available to read on many topics. There were lots of books on religion and even copies of the Bible were available in English rather than Latin. For the first time, ordinary men and women could read it for themselves instead of having to go to church and listen to what the priest told them. Some people who were not priests started to think very deeply about the Church and wonder whether everything they had ever been told was entirely correct.

Some people began to criticise the Church. These people still believed in God; they just felt that there might be different ways of worshipping him.

Criticism No. 1 — The Church was too rich!

▸ The Church owned about one-third of all the land in England. An ordinary peasant had to give 10% of their harvest (a tithe) to the priest every year. Some felt that the bishops, priests and monks lived in luxury whilst the poor suffered.

Criticism No. 2 — The priests didn't lead a very 'holy' life.

▸ Some priests had a few jobs and neglected their work. Villagers once told the Bishop of Hereford: 'The priest puts his horses and sheep in the churchyard … he was away for six weeks and made no arrangements for a substitute. Sir John (the priest) spends his time in the taverns and there his tongue is loosened to the scandal of everyone. He is living with a woman, Margaret, and he cannot read nor write and so cannot look after the parishioners' souls.' Ordinary people did not think some priests were setting a very good example to the people in the village or town.

Criticism No. 3 — Ordinary people couldn't understand the church services.

▸ The Bible was written in Latin and the church services were held in this language as well. People said they found it difficult to feel close to God if they couldn't understand what was being said in church.

Source A ▼ A print of the execution of William Tyndale. He was executed for translating the Bible into English so that ordinary people could read it.

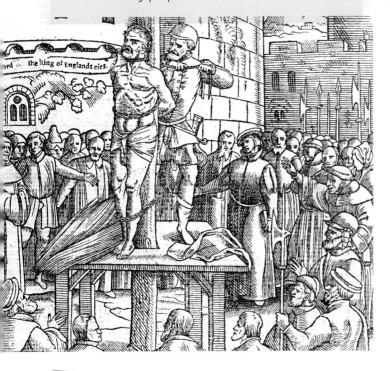

Source B ▼ Martin Luther painted by Cranach the Younger (1472–1553)

FACT: ▶ Catholics and Protestants

The Catholic way to worship

- The Pope is Head of the Catholic Church and is chosen by God.
- The Bible and prayer books are written in Latin.
- A church should be a bright and colourful place to worship God, with pictures on the walls, stained-glass windows, a large stone altar, silver cups and crosses, and priests in magnificent robes.

The Protestant way to worship

- A country's monarch should be the Head of the Church.
- The Bible and prayer books should be in a language that the worshippers understand – not in Latin.
- A church should be a plain and simple place to worship God. Money shouldn't be wasted on decorations or robes for the priest.

Criticism No. 4 **Poor people couldn't afford 'indulgences'.**

- When a person died, they went to heaven or hell. It was thought you passed through a place called purgatory on the way. In purgatory, people believed you were punished for any sins you may have committed whilst you were alive. It wasn't meant to be a nice place to stay for very long. When you were alive, you could buy 'indulgences' from a bishop. This meant that you travelled through purgatory quicker. Rich people could buy lots of indulgences. Poor people didn't think it was fair. They thought that they were being punished for being poor.

WISE UP WORDS

indulgences   purgatory   Protestants   tithe

In 1517, a German monk called Martin Luther wrote out a long list of criticisms of the Catholic Church and nailed it to his local church door. Luther wanted the Catholic Church to change and soon his ideas and beliefs attracted many followers. By 1529, the followers were known as **Protestants** because they protested against the Catholic Church. Now there were two religious groups in Europe who believed in a Christian version of God – the Catholics and the Protestants. However, both wanted to worship him in slightly different ways.

WORK

1 In your own words, explain why religion and the Church played such an important part in people's lives.

2 Explain the origin of the word 'Protestant'.

3 The year is 1517. Imagine you are Martin Luther, angry with the Catholic Church. Using the information on these pages to help you, write your own list of criticisms of the Church. You could try and make your work look old – ask your teacher for advice on how to do this.

HISTORY MYSTERY

Why did the Mary Rose sink?

The Mary Rose was Henry VIII's favourite warship, built in 1511 and named after Henry's younger sister, Mary, and the famous Tudor symbol, a rose. Over 90 cannon were packed on board and she also carried hundreds of soldiers armed with swords, daggers, longbows and arrows.

On 19 July 1545, England was facing a huge French invasion fleet. Henry VIII stood watching them from Southsea Castle, near Portsmouth. His latest warship – the Mary Rose – appeared in view and sailed towards the French. The crew fired their cannons a few times, the ship turned and then... disaster! It began to sink. There was panic on board as men began to scramble to get off the sinking ship. Many of her crew couldn't swim and over 400 of them drowned.

The French invasion itself was a failure but the French soon claimed a victory of sorts – they said they had sunk the Mary Rose. Marshal du Bellay, a Frenchman, wrote:

'Fortune followed our fleet. The Mary Rose, one of their best ships, was sunk by our cannon and of the five or six hundred men which were on board, only five and thirty escaped.'

So was this true? Did the French sink the Mary Rose? If not, then why did she sink? It is time to be a History Mystery detective, so study the evidence very carefully.

EVIDENCE A

'There are no gaping holes in the ship where a French shot might have hit... but we've only got half a ship, so we can't say any damage happened in any other place. We don't know what damage might have been done.'

Alexzandra Hildred, a marine expert, talking after analysing the ship. In 1982, the ship was brought back up to the surface and preserved in a museum.

EVIDENCE B

'To sink a ship like this with one or two hits would be astonishing.'

Professor Andrew Lambert, a historian.

EVIDENCE C

'When the Mary Rose sank in 1545, she had all the latest weapons on board... was the ship too heavy and unstable? Our experts have worked out that the weight of the new guns had made the ship unstable... but the weight alone was not enough to sink her.'

From a TV documentary broadcast in 2003 about the Mary Rose.

EVIDENCE D

'There were 700 men aboard ship. The usual crew of 415 plus 300 heavily armed soldiers were concentrated in the bow and the stern [front and back of the ship]. I saw the ship heel over as she turned and only 36 were saved.'

Part of a letter written by Sir Peter Carew, younger brother of Sir George Carew. George was on board, in charge of the ship when it sank.

EVIDENCE E

'New **gun-ports** were cut, low down, in each side of the *Mary Rose* to take big guns. It was hard to make them watertight. It seemed odd to be cutting holes low in the side of a ship. I remember saying that I hoped the ship would not lean over with its gun holes left open.'

Written by one of the men who helped to cut the new gun-ports in 1536.

EVIDENCE F

'When the archaeologist recovered the *Mary Rose*, all the main gun-ports were fitted with lids. To their surprise, the lids were bound [tied] open, indicating that they could have been open when she sank.'

From a TV documentary broadcast in 2003 about the *Mary Rose*.

EVIDENCE G

'The ship faced towards the harbour when she was discovered. Her position, in conjunction with the evidence from the guns recovered, suggests she sank as she was executing a turn while engaging the enemy.'

From the archaeologists' report after the ship was recovered in 1982.

EVIDENCE H

'According to English sources of the time, the *Mary Rose* capsized accidentally because of the negligence or lack of discipline of her crew. Sir George Carew... on board the *Mary Rose* was asked why the ship was leaning to one side. He replied, "I have the sort of knaves [mischievous men] I cannot rule." Soon after this the *Mary Rose* leaned even further over as water poured through open gun-ports and she sank rapidly.'

From the book 'The Mary Rose' (1981).

WISE UP WORDS

unstable   negligence   gun-ports

WORK

Well then history detective, now you have the difficult task of working out why the *Mary Rose* sank.

You must search through all the evidence and work out your theory. Here are some of the main theories for you to consider.

1 The French sank her.

2 The ship was too heavy and unstable.

3 The crew were unruly and would not follow orders.

4 The gun-ports were left open.

First – Find any evidence that the French sank the ship.
Does any evidence support the French claim? Can you find any evidence that shows this theory to be unlikely? What is your opinion? Make a note of your findings.

Second – Find evidence that the ship was too heavy or unstable.

Does any evidence support this idea? If it was heavy and unstable, why was it so? Write down what you have discovered.

Third – Think – could the open gun-ports have sunk the *Mary Rose*?
Find evidence to support this theory. Why might they have been left open? Could the crew's behaviour have anything to do with it? Why were the gun-ports so low in the water in the first place? Make notes on the evidence you have found.

Finally – You must deliver your verdict. Why did the *Mary Rose* sink?

Write a short paragraph to outline your theory as to why the *Mary Rose* sank on the 19 July 1545. Be sure to use some of the evidence you have found to back up your ideas. Why don't you imagine that you were writing the report for Henry VIII?

Edward VI: the boy king

AIMS
- ▶ How and why did Henry's son Edward change England?
- ▶ What sort of boy was the boy king?

Despite all his marriages, Henry VIII only had three children by the time he died on 28 January 1547. Edward was nine, Elizabeth was 14 and Mary was an adult of 31. Henry had absolutely no doubt as to who would run the country after he died… Edward of course! The young prince may only have been nine years old but he was a male. His two sisters were older than him but they were women and Henry believed that a woman was not able to rule the country.

Changes in religion

As you have learned, Henry VIII had made some important changes to religion. He had closed all the monasteries (and taken their money), allowed the Bible to be read in English (not Latin) and most importantly, made himself, and future kings and queens, Head of the Church of England (instead of the Pope). Henry didn't make any more major changes to religion and most people, including the King, still thought of themselves as Catholic. However, Henry's son Edward believed deeply in the Protestant faith. As a Protestant, he thought that the Catholic Church made people worship God in the wrong way. He felt that God should be worshipped in a plain and simple manner. As he was Head of the Church, he could alter it in any way he wished. Once again, religion in England was about to change!

Many people, especially in the countryside, didn't like all the changes to the way they worshipped. They loved the old services and churches, and in some areas there were rebellions. The leaders of one rebellion in Cornwall saw just how ruthless young King Edward could be… he sent in his soldiers to hang the rebels from the nearest trees.

Edward had always been a sickly child and constantly in need of a doctor's attention. He used to have his bedroom walls washed down three times a day to keep him free from disease. But by the age of 15, he was dying of a lung disease called **tuberculosis**. His hair fell out, his nails came off and his fingers and toes began to loosen and drop away at the joints. Edward died on 6 July 1553. He had no children so his older sister, Mary, became the new Queen. She was a deeply religious Catholic. Protestant England was about to change.

Source A ▼ Inside a Catholic church

Rood screen (to separate priest from worshippers)

Sanctuary lamps

Gold crosses, candlesticks and chalices

Stained glass

Statue of Virgin Mary

Pictures to explain Bible stories

Stone alter

Expensive robes

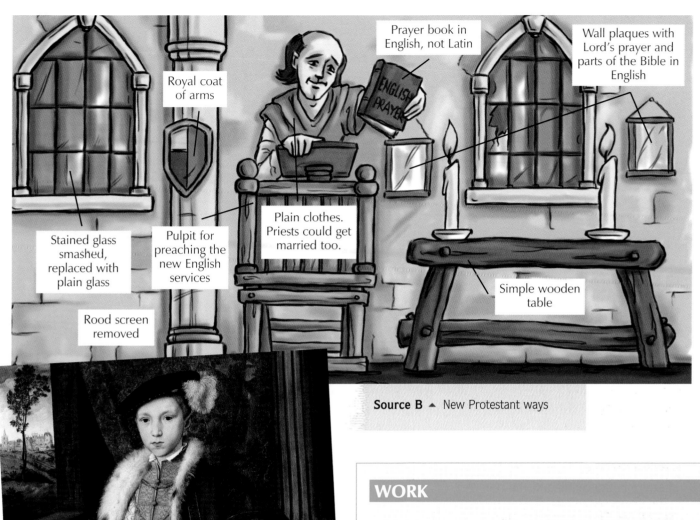

Royal coat of arms

Prayer book in English, not Latin

Wall plaques with Lord's prayer and parts of the Bible in English

Stained glass smashed, replaced with plain glass

Pulpit for preaching the new English services

Plain clothes. Priests could get married too.

Rood screen removed

Simple wooden table

Source B ▲ New Protestant ways

Source C ▲ A painting of Edward VI, painted in about 1550

FACT: ▶ Wicked Ed

▶ King Edward VI could be a cruel and vicious boy. He once executed his uncle for accidentally killing his favourite pet.

 WISE UP WORDS

tuberculosis   obituary

WORK

1 Why do you think Edward became King after his father's death and not Mary or Elizabeth?

2 Of all the changes made to religion by Edward and Henry, which do you think had the biggest effect on ordinary people's lives? Remember to explain the reasons for your answer.

3 Design and write an **obituary** for King Edward VI – an obituary briefly tells of some of the most important events, achievements and the personality of the person who recently died. Begin with Edward's birth on 12 October 1537 and end with his death on 6 July 1553 at the age of just 15.

HUNGRY FOR MORE?

Close to his death, Edward named his 16-year-old cousin, Lady Jane Grey, as next in line to the throne. She later became known as the 'Nine days queen'.
- *Who was she?*
- *Why did Edward choose her?*
- *How did she get her nickname?*
- *What happened to her?*

How 'bloody' was 'Bloody Mary'?

▶ How did 'Bloody Mary' get her nickname?
▶ Did she deserve it?

Do you or any of your friends have nicknames? If so, what are they and what are the reasons behind them? Mary I, Queen of England and Wales from 1553 to 1558, had a nickname – 'Bloody Mary'. Why? These pages will ask you to look at some evidence about her reign to see how she acquired her nasty nickname. Did she deserve it?

Mary I

When she became Queen in 1553, Mary was unmarried, 37 years old and a devout Catholic. Some people were delighted to have Mary as Queen. They didn't like all the religious changes that had taken place in Edward's reign. They looked forward to a time when Mary would bring back the old Catholic ways.

Mary married the Catholic King Philip of Spain, but this was seen as a bad move. Philip and the Spanish were very unpopular in England. Would this Spanish King interfere in the running of the country?

As soon as she was crowned, Mary started to undo all the changes her father and brother had made:

- England was officially a Catholic country once more.
- The Pope was the Head of the English and Welsh Churches again.
- The churches were redecorated – stone altars, bright painted walls, statues, gold crosses and candlesticks were added.
- Married priests were made to leave their wives.
- Church services and prayer books were in Latin once more.

Mary's changes didn't please the Protestants who were becoming fed up of this religious see-saw. Her message to them was simple – change religion or be punished! You might now see how Mary acquired her nickname.

Source A ▾ A painting of Bloody Mary

'I will spare the life of Lady Jane.'

Source C ▲ Lady Jane Grey was named Queen by the previous King, Edward VI. She didn't last long at all. Mary's troops marched into London and arrested her. Mary promised not to kill Jane but soon ordered the execution of 16-year-old Jane, her husband and other family members!

Source D ▾ From 'History Alive 1 1485–1714', by Peter Moss (1980)

'About 300 people were burned to death all over the country because they refused to worship the Catholic way. Most of these were humble shopkeepers, carpenters, farmers and housewives.'

Source B ▾ From a letter written at the time, celebrating the arrival of the new Queen

'All the people of London rejoiced and made many great fires. They set out tables and feasted. The bells rang till ten of the clock at night.'

Source E ▾ The burning of Latimer and Ridley, two Protestants who refused to become Catholics

Source H ▾ From a letter written at the time of Mary's death

'...when Mary died, all the churches of London did ring, and at night did make bonfires and set tables in the street and did eat and drink and be merry...'

Source F ▾ From a book called 'Book of Martyrs' by John Fox, a Protestant. A **martyr** is someone who is prepared to die for what they believe in.

'There were burnt 5 bishops, 21 ministers, 8 gentlemen, 84 workers, 100 farmers, servants and labourers, 26 wives, 20 widows, 9 girls, 2 boys and 2 infants.'

! WISE UP WORD

martyr

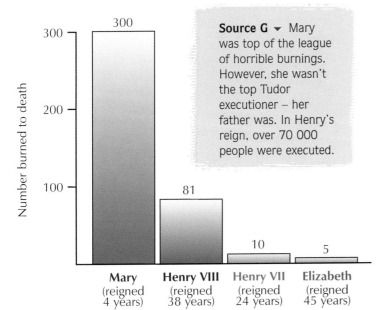

Source G ▾ Mary was top of the league of horrible burnings. However, she wasn't the top Tudor executioner – her father was. In Henry's reign, over 70 000 people were executed.

Number burned to death

Mary (reigned 4 years)	300
Henry VIII (reigned 38 years)	81
Henry VII (reigned 24 years)	10
Elizabeth (reigned 45 years)	5

WORK

1 Read **Source B**.

a How did the people of London react to the news that Mary was their new Queen?

b Why do you think they were so happy?

c **Sources B** and **H** were written by the same person. How had public opinion about their Queen changed during Mary's time as Queen?

d Why do you think opinions changed? You might like to use **Sources C, D** and **E** to help you with your answer.

2 a List five examples of actions that would have made Mary unpopular with the majority of the Protestant English.

b From your list, choose one example that you think would have had the worst effect on Mary's popularity. Explain why you have chosen this as your example.

3 Read **Source F**.

a Why might you not be able to trust everything that is written in Fox's book?

b Do you think this book was published during Mary's reign? Give reasons for your answer.

The nastiest nursery rhyme in the world!

▶ What does the famous nursery rhyme 'Mary, Mary, quite contrary' really mean?
▶ What does this rhyme tell us about Mary's life?

You've all heard it. Most of you will have sung it. Mothers sing it to babies; children sing it in nursery classes and pupils sing it in the playground. It sounds like a nice friendly rhyme about a girl called Mary. But would you sing it if you really knew what each line was about? The poem is about someone called Mary, but she's not a little girl. The Mary in the rhyme is 'Bloody Mary', Queen from 1553 to 1558 and famous for ordering the burning of over 300 Protestants.

Read through the poem carefully and then look through the fact boxes on these pages. Try to match them with each line. Prepare to be astonished! After you have read these pages you might think twice about singing it again.

Mary, Mary, quite contrary,

How does your garden grow?

With silver bells

And cockleshells,

And pretty maids all in a row.

Pregnant... or not?

Mary longed for a baby. She was delighted when she thought she was pregnant soon after marrying her husband, King Philip of Spain. However, she soon found out that she wasn't pregnant at all; her stomach pains were in fact the symptoms of a terrible disease, possibly cancer. One line of the rhyme **ridicules** the fact that nothing will grow inside her.

Changing her mind

'Contrary' means 'opposite'. If a person is contrary, it often means that they take a different view just for the sake of it. Mary was accused of being awkward by wanting to change England back to a Catholic country so soon after it had become a Protestant one.

King Philip of Spain – the love rat

Mary's husband wasn't very loving. King Philip hardly ever saw her during their marriage. Also, he had affairs with lots of other women. In Tudor England, this was called **cuckolding**. Which line do you think this is referring to?

A poor taste in music

Mary enjoyed listening to the sound of church bells. This music was unfashionable at the time.

Source A ▾ A portrait of Mary and Philip

Problems in childbirth

Mary was rumoured to have had some children, but each little girl was **stillborn** – Mary was supposed to have had them buried secretly in a long row of graves.

Have you worked it out? Can you match the five fact boxes to the five lines of the poem? Can you see how cruel the rhyme is? It must have been made up by someone who really hated Mary. What you thought was a harmless nursery rhyme about a girl called Mary was really a hateful, spiteful rhyme about an awkward woman with an **adulterous** husband, stillbirth, and the desire for a child, based on gossip and hearsay.

This isn't the only cruel or nasty nursery rhyme. 'Jack and Jill' doesn't have a very happy ending, 'Rock a bye baby' ends in disaster and as for poor old 'Humpty Dumpty'! And we sing all of these to little babies. Try to find out more about some famous nursery rhymes. 'Ring a Ring a Roses', 'Humpty Dumpty' and 'Little Jack Horner' all have fascinating stories surrounding them.

> ## ! WISE UP WORDS
> ridicule adulterous cuckolding stillborn

WORK

1 a Copy out each line of the nursery rhyme, but leave a few blank spaces underneath each line.

   b Underneath each line, explain what it *really* means in your own words.

2 Do you think the writer of the rhyme was a Protestant or a Catholic? Explain your answer.

3 This rhyme was once described as a 'lot of old, nasty gossip'. What do you think this means? Explain your answer carefully.

4 Imagine you are the person who wrote the poem. Try to justify why you wrote such a spiteful poem. Use what you have learned about Mary to help you.

5 Why do you think nursery rhymes were so common in Tudor and Stuart times?

Have you been learning?

Task 1

The passage below doesn't make sense. It needs capital letters, commas and full stops. Some words are spelt incorrectly. (In total, five words are spelt incorrectly.)

Copy the passage, making corrections as you write.

> leonardo da vinci was a genious he tried hard to be the best at everything he did he filled his days with things to do such as studying fossels oil painting glass making and wepon building leonardo was especially concerned with a dream of flying and dreamed of designing a machine that wood allow a man to fly like a bird the period in which leonardo lived was known as the rennasance.

Task 2

a Can you work out who is in the picture below?

b Write a sentence or two about each of the people pictured with Henry VIII.

c Could all five people have stood together to have this picture painted? Think carefully about your answer.

Source A ▾ Painting of Henry VIII, his three children and Jane Seymour

Task 3

Note making is an important skill. To do it successfully you must pick out any key words in each of the sentences. In other words, without these key words the sentence would make no sense. The first one has been done for you.

a   In **1485, Henry VII** was **crowned** the **King of England**. The key words are 1485, Henry VII, crowned and King of England.

b   At this time most people thought that the world was flat.

c   The only areas that were really known about were Europe, the Holy Land, northern Africa and the Eastern lands, such as China and India.

d   By 1500, many explorers had read the stories of the famous adventurer Marco Polo.

e   Ptolemy, a Greek writer, wrote a book entitled *Geography* in which he talked of the theory that the world was not flat but shaped like a ball.

f   Several brave explorers, including Christopher Columbus, became excited by the stories of adventure and decided to sail further than they had sailed before.

g   They were helped by accurate compasses, top quality sails and good rudders.

Top Tip: Note making is an important skill to use during revision time. Can you make notes on any other paragraphs in your books?

Task 4

Here are six groups of words. In each group there is an odd one out. When you have found it, write a sentence or two to describe why you think it doesn't fit in.

a   Queen Isabella • Amerigo Vespucci • Ferdinand Magellan • John Cabot

b   Tobacco • Tomatoes • Potatoes • Cabbage • Cocoa

c   Tower • Rack • Boot • Press

d   Edward • Henry • Elizabeth • Mary

e   Catherine of Aragon • Anne Boleyn • Jane Seymour • Catherine Howard

f   Stained Glass • Silver Candlesticks • White Walls • Latin Bible

Task 5

Of all the characters you have met so far, who is most likely to have said the following? Copy each one into your book and write down the person whom you think may have said it. Then say why you think this.

a   'I wonder what it would be like to fly like a bird.'

b   'God will keep us safe. I promise you, we'll see land soon.'

c   'Land Ahoy.'

d   'I should never have worn that crown.'

e   'Money is no object when there's fun to be had.'

f   'Please forgive me darling, I don't want to die.'

g   'He may be a relative, but my favourite pet is dead.'

Task 6

a   Can you find the hidden words in the grid below? Your teacher will be able to make you a copy.

Independent • Spices • Martyr • Negligence • Genius • Indulgences • Population • Pope • Catholic • Native • Sphere • Explorer

I	N	D	E	P	E	N	D	E	N	T
N	A	L	U	O	W	E	O	D	A	B
D	A	B	S	P	I	C	E	S	T	E
U	G	I	P	U	U	E	I	X	I	G
L	E	X	P	L	O	R	E	R	V	A
G	S	F	M	A	R	T	Y	R	E	S
E	A	C	A	T	H	O	L	I	C	P
N	E	G	L	I	G	E	N	C	E	H
C	O	E	X	O	I	A	P	O	P	E
E	H	G	E	N	I	U	S	H	P	R
S	G	I	J	O	E	U	T	S	J	E

b   When you have located each word, write a sentence or two to explain what each word means.

Rich man, poor man

AIMS
▸ What were the four main social groups in Tudor society?
▸ What were the differences between rich and poor Tudors?

We are all different. We all look, dress and behave differently. We don't all have the same amount of money either. It was just the same in Tudor England. You could place people into groups. Historians often use the word **class** instead of group. In 1586, a man called William Harrison wrote a book called Description of England. In it, he divided people into four classes. He wrote, 'We in England divide our people into four groups: **gentlemen**, **citizens**, **yeomen** and **labourers**.' So what did he mean?

Now read about the four groups. Later on you will be asked to match each group to a house, a description of their life and a picture.

Who were the **gentlemen**?

These guys were rich. Some were very, very rich like the dukes and earls. They lived in huge country houses with lots of rooms in which to hold dinner parties, dances, plays and music concerts. They employed servants to look after them. Other gentlemen were not quite so rich but still lived in large houses with plenty of land. Gentlemen (and their wives and families) made up about 5% of the population.

Who were the **citizens**?

These people lived in towns and were still rich. Some made money from buying and selling goods, such as wool, jewellery, food, wine or cloth. These men were sometimes called **merchants**. They lived in fine townhouses and had servants. They made up about 5% of the population.

Who were the **yeomen**?

They were farmers. They either owned their own land or rented land from a gentleman. They often lived in a medium-sized farmhouse and made quite a good living from farming crops (wheat or barley, for example) or cattle, pigs or sheep. They employed people to work on their farms and some yeomen even had servants. Yeomen and their families made up about 30% of the population.

Who were the **labourers**?

These people were similar in status to the peasants of the Middle Ages. If they lived in the country – and most did – they would work on a farm. Some had their own small piece of land to grow their own vegetables and keep a few chickens. Some labourers lived in towns and might have worked as carpenters, tailors, shoemakers or bricklayers. Labourers made up about 60% of the population.

Source A ▾ Home A

Source B ▾ Home B

Source D ▾ Home D

Source C ▾ Home C

Description 1

'He eats well: bread, beer and beef, good food … full bellyfuls. He works hard: making hay, shearing corn, his workers are happy to farm for him.'

Description 2

'His house has walls of earth, a low thatched roof, few rooms … a hole in the wall to let out smoke … he is very poor and has to labour hard for his living.'

Description 3

'Every day he wears silks, velvets, satins and such like. He once gave away a pair of perfumed gloves with 24 small gold buttons, in each button a small diamond.'

Description 4

'He brought back with him wine, olive oil, currants, silk, clothes and dates. He sold them to a man who then sold them in London.'

Picture 1

Picture 2

Picture 3

Picture 4

FACT: ▸ The lowest of the low

▸ Even lower than the poorest labourers were the **paupers** – people who had no jobs and relied on charity. Some paupers were given permission to beg and wore special badges to show this. Others went to their local church to collect 'relief' – a few pennies to buy clothes or bread. Local people were taxed to pay for this.

In 1601, a **Poor Law** put the paupers into four categories. Each group was treated differently:

1. Pauper children – given work.
2. Sick paupers – looked after in special homes.
3. Fit paupers – given work (they received food and drink as payment).
4. Lazy, idle paupers – whipped, then sent to a House of Correction (a place where they were forced to work, then their products were sold).

Again, people were taxed to pay for the relief provided through the Poor Law.

FACT: ▸ Tudor traders

▸ Some merchants made vast fortunes from forming trading companies. For example, the East India Company, set up in 1600, sent huge ships to India to collect valuable cargos of spices, silk, jewels, ivory and carpets. When arriving back in England, these goods were sold for massive profits.

WISE UP WORDS

merchant   yeoman   pauper   gentleman
labourer   citizen   Poor Law   class

WORK

1 In your own words, explain the meaning of the following:

   Gentleman • Citizen • Yeoman • Labourer
   • Pauper

2 a Copy this chart carefully.

   b Complete the chart by looking closely at the information on these pages. Match the descriptions and pictures to the correct group or 'class' of people.

c Now choose one of the sets of sources you have matched together and explain how you made your decision, for example:

   • I think picture _____ shows a gentleman because…

   • Home _____ would belong to a gentleman because…

   • Description _____ is that of a gentleman because…

Class	Which **home** do you think he lived in? (A–D)	Which **description** matches him?	What does he look like? Choose from pictures 1–4.
Gentleman Citizen Yeoman Labourer			

Punishment and torture

▶ How were some crimes punished in Tudor and Stuart England?
▶ How did some torture instruments work?

There were some brutal punishments in Tudor and Stuart England.

- In 1533, a cook was boiled to death in a cauldron for poisoning the Bishop of Rochester. Five years later, Margaret Bowmer was tied to a post and burned alive for being married to two men at once.

- In 1522, a man had the letter 'F' branded on his cheek, his ears were sliced off, his nostrils were slit open and his hands were cut off. He had been caught stealing.

- Beggars were regularly put in the pillory and whipped until their backs were ribboned flesh. A hole would be burned through their ear the first time they were caught. The other ear would be 'holed' next time. If they were caught a third time they would be hanged.

There was no police force in Tudor and Stuart times. Instead, **Justices of the Peace** were officially appointed by the government to keep law and order in towns and villages. They might try to investigate crimes and gather information but they were very busy with other duties. They had to look after the roads and bridges, check on the alehouses, report people who didn't go to church and much more. A way of saving time and gaining information or evidence was to use **torture**.

The Rack

How did it work? A strong iron frame about two metres long with rollers at each end. The victim's hands and feet were tied to the rollers. As the rollers were turned in opposite directions, the victim was stretched.

FACT: ▶ Knives out for Fawkes

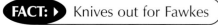

▶ Guy Fawkes was tortured on the rack, the only one in England at the time. His arms and legs were probably dislocated by the time he made a full confession. A famous Tudor torturer boasted that his victims were a foot longer by the time he had finished with them.

The Boot

How did it work? A victim's foot was placed in a heavy metal boot. Slowly, wooden wedges were hammered down the sides. Gradually the anklebones would be crushed and splintered into pieces.

FACT: ▶ Which foot?

▶ The torture was mainly used on people accused of being witches.

Thumbscrews

How did it work? The victim's thumbs were placed between two metal bars. The bars were slowly screwed together, gradually crushing the thumbs.

FACT: ▶ Fingers and thumbs

▶ Thumbscrews were the first type of handcuffs. Instead of their wrists being handcuffed together like today, a prisoner was 'thumb cuffed' instead!

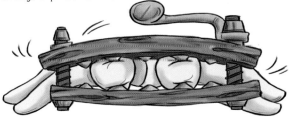

Skeffington's Irons

How did it work? The prisoner was ordered to curl himself up into a ball. Pieces of iron were placed around him. The irons were tightened with a screw. Either the prisoner owned up to the crime… or his back was broken.

FACT: ▶ Scary Skeffington

▶ It was named after its inventor Leonard Skeffington. He was in charge of torture weapons for Henry VIII.

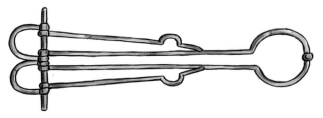

PAUSE FOR THOUGHT

A torturer's aim was to get the prisoner to confess to their crimes, after which they would be punished. By looking at these weapons of torture, it's little wonder that hundreds of people owned up… probably to crimes they had never even committed. We will never know how many innocent people were tortured and punished, they just owned up because the torture hurt so much.

The Press

How did it work? A prisoner was forced to lie on the floor and a strong wooden board was laid on top of them. One by one, heavy stones or metal weights were put on top of the board, squashing the victim underneath. The prisoner was continually asked to own up to their crime. Failing to do so meant another heavy weight would be placed on top of them.

FACT: ▶ Impressive press

▶ A famous Tudor torturer once wrote, 'I knew he would last no longer when I heard his chest crack.'

WISE UP WORDS

Justice of the Peace   torture

WORK

1 Explain the job of Justice of the Peace.

2 a Do you think torture was a fair method of getting people to confess to their crimes? Give reasons for your answer.

   b Why do you think torture is illegal throughout most of the world today? List as many reasons as you can.

   c If you were able to ask a Tudor king or queen why torture was needed, what answer might they have given?

3 Most of this torture equipment still survives today, kept on display in the Tower of London. Design an information leaflet for a young schoolchild to use as a guide on a torture chamber tour. Include:
   • Colourful pictures of the torture instruments
   • Facts about how they worked
   • A background to torture
   • An imaginative title, for example, 'The Tower's Terrible Torture Guide'

What were Tudor schools like?

AIMS

‣ How were people educated in Tudor England?

‣ How are Tudor schoolrooms different from today's modern classrooms?

A Tudor child's education often depended on how wealthy their father was. Poor families couldn't afford school fees so their children started work when they were about five or six years old. Richer families might send their children to a **grammar school**, so called because they taught mainly Latin and Greek grammar.

The following scene is based on a school near Chester called Banbury Grammar School, which opened in 1594.

1 **School Rules**: Tudor schools were very strict. You could be beaten for being late, not learning to spell properly, swearing, making fun of another pupil, forgetting books or gambling. Are some of your school rules similar to the ones Tudor children had to follow?

2 **The Birch**: A bundle of birch twigs or even a whip were used to hit children. A punishment session would be held once a week! Some school badges actually showed boys being caned. Why do you think that this type of punishment has stopped in the last 50 years?

3 **A Portrait**: A painting of the king, queen or the man who founded the school would often be displayed in the classroom. Does your school display any portraits or photographs of any important people?

4 **Printed Books**: Each pupil was expected to bring their own Bible at Banbury Grammar School. Why do you think that many of the other books were kept behind the teacher?

5 **Girls in School**: Girls were allowed to study at Banbury until they were nine, or until they had learned to read. It wasn't common to see girls in a classroom and many were educated at home. Some free places were also allocated to boys who were poor but clever.

6 **Lesson Time**: What lesson do you think is taking place here? What makes you think this? Children wrote with a **quill pen**, made from a feather and often read out loud from a **hornbook** (it looks like a bat). What else do you think it could be used for? One side would have the alphabet and the Lord's Prayer on it. The other side was left blank and was used to practise writing or maths on.

7 **Teacher**: Sometimes called a schoolmaster. Teachers were always men and could be very strict. In one school, a particularly strict teacher used to whip pupils every morning in winter… just to warm himself up!

8 **Toys**: Balls, spinning tops and hoops were used at break times. The pupils would usually have two or three breaks each day, bringing bread, beef and beer with them from home. The day would begin at 6:00am and home time could be twelve hours later.

! WISE UP WORDS

quill pen   hornbook   birch   grammar school

WORK

1 Write two sentences to describe each of the following:
birch • quill pen • hornbook

2 Why did so few poor children go to school in Tudor times?

3 Make a list of five similarities and five differences between your school and a school in Tudor times.

4 'A day in the life of __name__ at __name__ Grammar School.'

Imagine you are a pupil at the Tudor version of your school. Using the information provided on these pages, write a diary entry describing a typical day at your school.

Based on a cartoon by Dai Owen

HUNGRY FOR MORE?

Using your local library, find out details of the oldest school in your area.
- *How old is it?*
- *How has the school changed over the years?*
- *Are there any things that have stayed the same and provide us with evidence of the past?*
- *Are there any famous ex-pupils?*

How did people have fun in Tudor England?

AIMS
‣ How was Tudor entertainment different from modern entertainment?
‣ How horrible were Tudor fun and games?

There was no television or radio in Tudor times. People couldn't go to the cinema, play on a computer game or listen to CDs. Instead, they had to make their own entertainment. You will easily recognise some of the games and sports... others might leave you reaching for the sick bucket!

Go to public executions: Tudor people loved to see criminals being killed. Poorer criminals were hung; richer ones were beheaded with a sword. In London, spectators complained when one hangman executed 20 people at once – they were not happy because they wanted the criminals to be killed one at a time so they could see the expression on each prisoner's face!

Join in with the football match: One village or town would take on another. The ball (a pig's bladder full of sawdust and peas) would be carried, kicked and thrown across the land between the two villages. The winning 'team' was the one that got the ball into the centre of the other village. In 1602, a spectator wrote, 'The players go home as if they have been at war – bleeding heads, bones broken and out of joint, and such bruises as serve to shorten their days.'

Play Cudgels or Shin-hacks: Two simple games for two players.

To play Cudgels – two people stand opposite each other, each holding a heavy stick. They then take it in turns to hit each other. The person left standing wins.

To play Shin-hacks – two people stand opposite each other in their biggest, heaviest boots. They take it in turns to kick each other as hard as they can. The person left standing wins.

Watch the strolling players: Groups of actors travelled from village to village and acted out well-known stories or plays. They also carried news and gossip. Often, they were joined by acrobats, jugglers, musicians and puppeteers. Plays soon became so popular that special theatres were built. William Shakespeare wrote plays that were performed in the Globe Theatre in London.

Bet on blood sports: A bear or a bull would be tied to a post and attacked by a pack of wild dogs. Sometimes two cocks or chickens would be forced to attack each other after having their beaks sharpened and metal blades attached to their legs. People would bet on the results. Some successful bears, such as Harry Hunks, Tom Lincoln and Blind Robin, became as famous as some footballers and pop stars are today.

All the fun of the fair: There were no roller coaster rides or arcade games. Instead, a fair was a large noisy market full of goods to buy, food to eat and entertainment to watch (or join in with). Fire-eaters, tightrope walkers, sword fighting and dog racing were all popular, as were most of the other sports and entertainment on this page.

FACT: ▶ Famous fairs

▶ London – Cloth Fair

Nottingham – Goose Fair

Birmingham – Gingerbread Fair

Gloucester – 'Cotswold Olimpicks', a week of noise, food, fun and fighting

Why not try to find out about one of these? The Goose Fair is still going strong today.

FACT: ▶ Royal sports stars

▶ Kings and queens enjoyed sport too. Henry VIII enjoyed tennis, archery, skittles and wrestling. In 1520, he challenged King Francis of France to a wrestling match. The two men actually wrestled each other but Henry fell over and lost after a few minutes. He was so humiliated that he claimed he had been tripped up!

Mary Queen of Scots had her own billiards table and also enjoyed the odd game of golf – so did Charles I who played in a field near Newcastle a few months before he had his head chopped off.

FACT: ▶ Time for fun

▶ Most games, sports and festivals would take place on holy days such as Christmas, May Day and Midsummer Eve. People would attend church services in the morning and have fun later on in the day. The word 'holiday' comes from the words 'holy day'.

WISE UP WORDS

strolling players   blood sports
cudgelling   shin-hacking

WORK

1   a   Which forms of Tudor entertainment seem unpleasant or cruel to us or have been made illegal today?

    b   Why do you think some of the sports and entertainments have been banned?

2   a   Where does the word 'holiday' come from?

    b   Why would a band of strolling players coming to town be such a big event in Tudor times?

    c   In what ways is the modern game of football different to that played in Tudor times?

3   Design a poster advertising a local fair in Tudor times. Remember to include the day of the fair (it must be on the day of a religious festival) and details of the entertainment taking place.

And now for your Shakespeare lesson

 AIMS

▸ How did the theatre develop in Tudor England?
▸ Why is William Shakespeare seen as one of the world's greatest **playwrights**?

We've all heard of William Shakespeare. Most people will be able to name a few of the plays he wrote – Hamlet, Romeo and Juliet, Macbeth, A Midsummer Night's Dream. Many of his plays have even been made into movies starring famous film stars. But what has made this man so famous? Why do we still talk about him today, watch his plays and study his work at school?

Source A ▸
A picture of the Swan Theatre from c1596

A flag, a trumpet playing or a cannon firing announced the start of the play. In 1613, the Globe Theatre burned down when the cannon set the roof on fire.

The **galleries**

There was little scenery on stage, so the writer had to make sure that he told the audience exactly what was going on, including the time of day, the location and so on.

The **pit**

There were no female actors; all parts were played by men and boys.

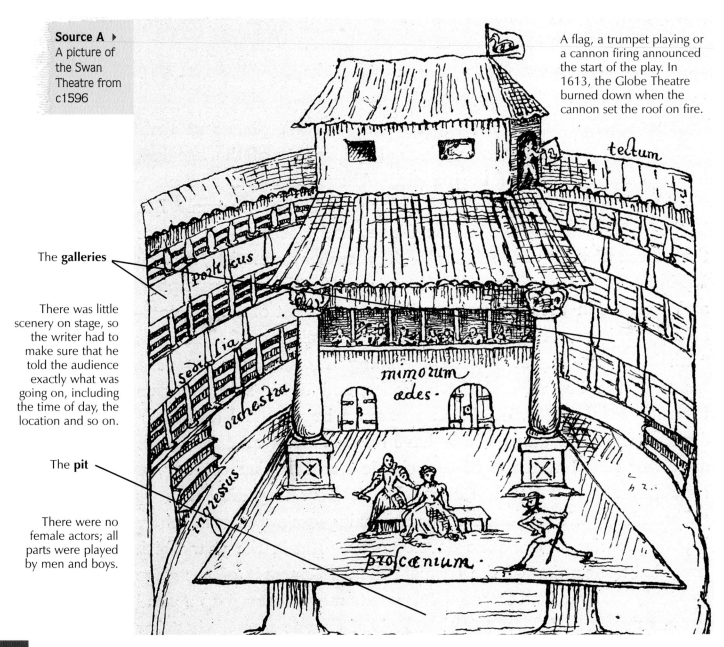

People loved watching plays in Tudor times and Queen Elizabeth was a big fan too. She would even command a group of actors to visit her palace and act for her. In 1576, an actor named James Burbage saw a chance to make some money from this and built the first permanent theatre in Shoreditch, just north of London.

THE THEATRE SHOREDITCH

Price List

Standing in the pit 1 Penny

Sitting in the gallery 2 Pennies

The best seats – with cushions

3 Pennies

- Theatres were round with no roofs.

- Plays were put on in the afternoon.

- Pies, beer, fruit and soup could be bought during the performance.

- Money was collected and stored in locked boxes. This is where we get the term 'box office'.

- Unlike today, theatres were often noisy, with audiences shouting, talking and laughing through the performance.

James Burbage made a fortune. Soon other theatres were built nearby, such as the Swan, the Fortune and the Globe. In the 1580s, an actor named William Shakespeare came to London to find work at the Globe... he fancied himself as a writer too.

Source B ▼ Flona Shaw – TV Presenter on BBC's Greatest Britons series

'Engineering gets us from A to B; Science helps us to understand what's around us; but Shakespeare does what no one else has done. He makes us understand our thoughts and feelings and what could be more useful in our lives than that?'

Source C ▼ This portrait, painted in 1610, is thought to be one of the most accurate of Shakespeare

Shakespeare as a playwright

Shakespeare is thought to have started writing plays in 1588. He wrote 37 in total and he sometimes appeared in them at his favourite theatre, the Globe. Like us today, the Tudor audiences probably didn't understand everything they heard on stage and must have been just as confused as we are. There are several major reasons for this:

1 The Tudors loved to make up new words. Shakespeare himself invented about 1700 new words, such as bandit, eyeball, elbow, lonely and leapfrog. Have you ever been called a 'tower of strength' or been 'tongue tied'? Has your pencil or pen ever vanished into 'thin air'? Have you ever puzzled over something and said, 'It's all Greek to me'? Shakespeare made up all of these phrases. We don't use all the words and phrases Shakespeare made up, so his writing can still cause confusion today.

2 Shakespeare wrote his plays to be acted, not just read, but he had to make sure that the audience knew exactly what was going on. This is why Shakespeare often wrote long descriptive passages to describe one scene. They tell of the time of day, the location and so on. He encourages the audience to use their imagination.

3 English people didn't all speak the same English. Shakespeare was from the Midlands and was born in Stratford-upon-Avon, near Birmingham and he probably had a 'brummie' accent. In London, people spoke differently, sometimes using different words and phrases. In his plays, Shakespeare uses both kinds of English, some of which we don't recognise any more.

Shakespeare 'for all time'

Shakespeare's plays are famous all over the world. They are important because they not only show us how people lived and thought in Tudor times, but also because he wrote about everyday human emotions, such as love, hate and jealousy. We still experience these feelings today and people can relate to them whatever century his plays are set in.

Ben Jonson, another famous Tudor writer, wrote that Shakespeare 'was not of an age, but for all time'. How many of today's playwrights will have their work studied in schools and acted out in theatres, cinema and on the TV in 400 years' time?

FACT: ▶ Would you dare to dig?

▸ The following words are engraved on Shakespeare's tombstone in Stratford-upon-Avon:

'Blest the man who spares these stones, and curst be he that moves my bones.'

Some people think that there might be an undiscovered play in his coffin... but no one has dared to dig down to find out – why?

! WISE UP WORDS

gallery   pit   playwright

WORK

1 a What was James Burbage's claim to fame?

   b Why do you think fewer people visit the theatre today than in Shakespeare's time?

2 a Describe the sights, sounds and smells that a visitor to the Globe Theatre in London would have experienced in Shakespeare's time.

   b How do Tudor theatre visits compare to visiting the theatre today?

3 Design a poster advertising one of Shakespeare's plays in London in the 1560s. (Remember to include: venue, date and time of production, entry cost, name of the play and perhaps even a few lines to encourage people to attend.)

4 Write a paragraph or two explaining why Shakespeare is regarded by many as one of the world's greatest playwrights. Think about his plays, popularity, influence on the English language and talent.

Crimewatch!

AIMS
▶ How did some criminals make money in Tudor England?
▶ What was 'canting'?

In Tudor England, some men and women were healthy and strong enough to work but found they could make more money from crime. They were known as '**sturdy beggars**' and they used lots of clever tricks to get money. They became a serious social problem.

Types of sturdy beggar

If caught committing crimes, sturdy beggars would receive harsh punishments. They could be tied to a post and whipped, branded with a hot iron bar, or forced to be slaves for a rich local man. Some were even executed.

• **The Clapperdudgeon**

He cut his skin to make it bleed and then tied dirty rags over the wound to make it look worse. He hoped that people would feel sorry for him and give him money.

• **The Cutpurse**

How do you think this criminal got his money?

• **The Baretop Trickster**

These women approached men and took off some of their clothes. They would trick men into buying them a meal – perhaps the man thought that he would get more than food... and usually he did! On the way to her home, he would be robbed by the woman and her gang of thieves.

• **The Soap Eater**

He would eat soap so that he would froth at the mouth. He would then pretend to have a fit. The worse he could make himself look, the more people would pity him and give him money.

• **Tom O'Bedlam**

This man pretended to be mad and do strange things. He might spend a few hours barking like a dog or walking around with a chicken's head sticking out of his ear. Why do you think people gave him money?

• **The Bristler**

A bristle was a loaded or crooked dice. It was specially weighted which meant that it fell on whichever number the bristler chose.

FACT: ▶ Other 'sturdy beggars'

▶ The Angler: fixed a hook to a long stick and stole clothes from windows.

The Leatherhead: a mugger who beat people up for money.

The Dummerer: pretended to be deaf and dumb, hoping people would feel sorry for him.

Priggers of prancers: horse thieves.

 WISE UP WORDS

sturdy beggars   canting

Sturdy beggars had their own language, a kind of slang. It was called **canting**. They used it to speak to other thieves on busy streets. Why do you think that they had their own secret language?

Here are some of the words they used:

autern – church	flick – thief
beak – magistrate	glaziers – eyes
bits – coins	greenman – field
booze – ale	ken – house
boosing ken – ale	lifts – stolen items
bung – purse	maunding – begging
cahrs – gallows	mort – woman
cloy – steal	nab – head
cony – victim	peck – food
couch a hogshead – go to sleep	pigeon holes – stocks
	prancer – horse
cuffin – man	ken – prison
cut – talk queer	rome – good
draw – pick a pocket	shrap – wine
duds – clothes	
stow you – shut up	
tip – give	
yarrum – milk	

WORK

1 The year is 1543 and you work as a printer in a large town. The Mayor has asked you to design a leaflet warning visitors about the dangers of sturdy beggars. Your warning leaflet should include details about some (or all) of the sturdy beggars mentioned on these pages and about how they might try to trick someone. Remember: It is a warning leaflet, so it needs to be bright, colourful and easy to read.

2 a Make up a conversation between two sturdy beggars who have just been caught committing crimes. The two beggars don't want anyone to know what they are talking about so use 'canting' whenever possible. What crime did they commit? How were they caught? Why did they do it? What punishment do they expect?

b Pass your conversation to a friend and see if they can translate it.

What did Queen Elizabeth look like?

▸ Why is it so hard to establish what Elizabeth *really* looked like?
▸ Why did she carefully control her royal portraits?

Our current monarch is known to millions of people all over the world. Her face is on television, in the newspapers and even on the money we use. Some people have even seen her in real life as she travels around Britain and the world. Her family life has even been made into a soap opera on American television. Many people today are fascinated by our royal family.

In the sixteenth century, ordinary people were also very interested in their Queen – Elizabeth I. However, there was no television or daily newspapers to show what she looked like. You might have been lucky enough to glimpse her face as she toured around but it was highly unlikely that an ordinary person would see her for real.

So that her people could know what she looked like, Elizabeth used paintings or portraits. However, Elizabeth was a wise Queen and she cleverly controlled pictures that the public saw to create an image of herself that would impress everyone. Lord Cecil, who worked for the Queen, once said:

'Many painters have done portraits of the Queen but none has shown her looks and charms. Therefore, she has asked people to stop doing portraits of her until a clever painter has finished one which all other painters can copy. Her majesty, in the meantime, forbids the showing of any portraits which are ugly, until they are improved.'

The Queen would have official portraits sent to artists to be copied. No other portraits were allowed. For years, the artist would copy these portraits every time an admirer wanted a portrait of the Queen.

Look at the following five portraits (**Sources A–E**) and see if you can match them to the descriptions (1–5).

Source A

Source B

Source C

Source D

Source E

'Her face is oblong, fair but wrinkled; her eyes small, yet black and pleasant; her nose is a little hooked; her lips narrow; and her teeth black. She wears false hair and that red; her hands are small, her fingers long and her height neither tall nor short.'

German visitor, 1598

French visitor, 1597

'On her head she wears a great red wig. Her face appears to be very aged. It is long and thin. Her teeth are yellow and unequal and there are less on the left than on the right. Many of them are missing and one cannot understand her easily when she speaks. She is tall and graceful.'

1 Painted in 1588, just after the Spanish had tried, and failed, to invade England. In the background, the artist has painted some wrecked Spanish ships. Elizabeth's hand is on a globe to show she is one of the most powerful people in the world.

2 Painted soon after she was crowned. Elizabeth was about 25 years old.

3 An engraving of Elizabeth, created shortly before her death. Notice the 'bags' under her eyes.

4 Painted when she was in her twenties. Look carefully at her dress; it is covered in eyes and ears. What do you think the message is here?

5 Painted when Elizabeth was in her sixties. She is wearing a wig here.

Important visitors to England who met Elizabeth probably saw a very different person to the lady we see in each of the paintings. Some of the following descriptions are even quite insulting. We must remember that the Queen was over 60 when they were written.

WORK

1 a Why would it be unlikely that an ordinary person would meet Elizabeth I?

b Why then, were portraits of the Queen so important for Elizabeth and her subjects?

2 a Select one of the portraits on these pages. In your own words, write a detailed description of Elizabeth from this picture.

b If Elizabeth herself were to read your description, would she be pleased with what you have written? Explain your answer.

c Which of the portraits (**Sources A–E**) do you think Elizabeth would be most pleased with? Explain your answer.

3 Explain why Elizabeth I didn't allow 'the showing of any portraits which are ugly'.

HUNGRY FOR MORE? *Why not draw or paint your own royal portrait? Try basing it on one of the descriptions on this page.*

There's something about Mary

AIMS

▶ Who was Mary Queen of Scots?

▶ How was she involved in a famous plot to kill Queen Elizabeth?

By 1568, Elizabeth had been Queen for ten years. She hadn't married and she hadn't any children. This meant that if she died, her cousin Mary, Queen of Scotland, would become Queen of England and Wales too.

Mary had a troubled past. She was known as a great beauty but had difficulty keeping her husbands! She was married to the King of France – who died in a freak riding accident. She then married an English Lord – who was strangled and blown up. Soon after this, she married the man who was suspected of murdering her second husband!

The Scots were suspicious of Mary's connection to her second husband's death and some rebelled against her. She was forced to give up her throne and stand aside as her young son, James, was made King of Scotland. In 1568, she ran away to England, perhaps hoping that her cousin, Queen Elizabeth, would take pity on her.

Mary immediately caused problems for Elizabeth. She was Catholic for a start and made no secret of the fact that she thought she should be Queen of England instead of Elizabeth. Some English Catholics even agreed with her. Elizabeth's solution was a harsh but typically clever one. She kept Mary a virtual prisoner until she could make up her mind what to do with her. In fact, Mary was kept in various houses and castles and imprisoned for the next 17 years.

The two women never actually met each other in this time but finally Elizabeth was forced to take action against Mary. She had committed the terrible crime of supporting a plan to kill the English Queen!

Babington's plot

In 1586, a young, rich Catholic man called Anthony Babington had a secret plan to kill Elizabeth. He would organise six men to kill the English Queen, rescue Mary from her prison and make her the new Queen of England. However, Babington needed to know if Mary liked the idea. He needed to contact her in prison.

He managed to get Mary's servants to hide secret letters in beer barrels that were taken to her room. The letters were written in code. Mary wrote back saying she agreed to the plan. In fact, Mary's servants didn't work for her at all, they worked for England's chief spy, Sir Francis Walsingham, who took the letters straight to Elizabeth.

...ΔαℇⓈΔI7ϴαⓈℇhα//αⓈℇ▽

ᴄₒ▽ℙℸ.ᴄsⱽⓈⓈOΛₒ▽//shiΔ∞ℳⓈℇ<u>ᴟ</u>

ℇ∞αlℙℾ◻shoⱽI//O8ɫαΔᴄ⊞ₒ-αⓈh8

ℇℙoⓈΔsⱽℙℇα⊞ⱽᴄℇ<u>ᴟ</u>ℇ∞ΙΔshoΛα2ϥ

oho8ⱽᴄℙℸⓈffϨΛαΔoℇⓈΔoℳℇΙℳɫαlⓈⓈ

◻Ιαh⊞ℇ▽ℳαℇℳ...

O	ɫ	Λ	⊞	α	◻	ϴ	∞	I	Λ	ᓂ	h	//	Ⓢ	▽	s	n	ℙ	Δ	ℇ	ᴄ
A	B	C	D	E	F	G	H	I	J	K	L	M	N	O	P	Q	R	S	T	U

ᴄ	ᴄₒ	7	8	9	2	3	4	<u>ᴟ</u>	Ⓢ	ℳ	σ
V	W	X	Y	Z	AND	FOR	THAT	OF	THE	ME	REPEAT LETTER

USED TO CONFUSE: ff ┌ ┘ ᓂ ◻

Source A ▶ This is the part of Mary's letter that led to her execution. Can you work out what she wrote? What does she mean?

Source B ▲ The execution of Mary Queen of Scots in February 1587. The axeman took at least three blows to cut her head off. It was said that her lips continued to move after her head was separated from her body – then her wig fell off!

When the code was broken, the message was clear: Mary was supporting a plan to kill the Queen. This was **treason**.

Despite all the evidence, Elizabeth still didn't want to have her cousin executed. Eventually, her secretary, Sir John Davidson, slipped the death warrant in among some papers she had to sign. Elizabeth pretended she didn't really know what she was signing, signed it, changed her mind, then tried to stop the execution. But she was too late. Mary Queen of Scots had already been executed.

WISE UP WORD

treason

WORK

1 a Why was Mary, Queen of Scotland, next in line to the English throne?

   b Explain why Mary ran away from Scotland to England.

2 When Mary arrived in England, Queen Elizabeth had three choices. Should she:

   • Send her back to Scotland?

   • Put her in prison?

   • Allow her to carry on with life in England?

   In your own words, write down the choice she made. Then explain why you think she didn't choose the other options.

3 a In your own words, explain how Sir Francis Walsingham arranged to trap Mary.

   b Why do you think Elizabeth hesitated over her decision to have Mary executed?

4 Using the code, write out three facts about Mary's life. Make each one short and simple. Pass your coded facts to a friend and see if they can work out what you have written.

Match of the day!

AIMS

▶ Why did England and Spain go to war in 1588?
▶ How was each side equipped and how did their battle tactics differ?

Few people had ever seen Philip II, King of Spain, so angry. It was the morning of 20 April 1587 and he had just received some shattering news. The most famous English 'sea dog' of all, Sir Francis Drake, had just sailed into Cadiz harbour in northern Spain and set fire to 30 of Spain's royal warships! Philip was furious but had other reasons to be mad with the English…

- For years, the English sailors had been stealing gold and silver from Spanish ships.
- Philip (a Catholic) had recently heard news that Mary Queen of Scots (another Catholic) had been executed by Elizabeth I. He thought that the people who had killed a Catholic queen should be punished.
- Philip was fighting to keep the Spanish Netherlands (now known as Holland and Belgium) under his control. However, the Dutch rebels were being helped by soldiers from another country – yes you've guessed it… England!

NEXT FIXTURE

The English Navy
Owner: Queen Elizabeth
Managers: Sir Francis Drake and Lord Howard

Vs

The Spanish Armada
Owner: King Philip II
Manager: The Duke of Medina Sidonia

Date: Summer 1588
Venue: The English Channel

The Spanish have a fantastic fleet and they're confident that they will beat the English. They even call themselves the 'invincible **Armada**'. They do have a problem though. Their commander, the Duke of Medina Sidonia, suffers from seasickness. Can you believe that? – a seasick sea captain!

By the summer of 1588, Philip's forces had recovered from Drake's attack on Cadiz and he had assembled one of the greatest fleets of warships the world had ever seen. There were 170 Spanish ships, known as an **armada**, many painted red and gold, which together covered an area of about 12km of sea. His aim for the fleet was simple – meet up with 20 000 ground troops at Calais, transport them to invade England and remove Elizabeth from the English throne. He would then turn Protestant England into a Catholic country once more.

The Spanish are 'ropers and raiders'. Their ships are like huge floating castles, but are clumsy to steer. So the Spanish **galleons** will try to sail alongside the enemy ships and tie themselves alongside with ropes and hooks. Then soldiers will jump onto the enemy ships and fight with swords, daggers and **muskets**. The heavy guns below decks will almost touch the other ships, and will blow holes in their sides.

An English galleon

A Spanish galleon

The English are 'speedy smashers'. Their experienced sailors should be able to avoid any enemy attempts to get alongside. Instead, they will hope to position their ships 150m away and use their superior guns to first fire huge solid 20kg cannonballs through the side of the enemy ships. Then the smaller cannons known as 'man killers' will fire 8kg balls at the sailors. When the Spanish ships are floating wrecks packed with battered and tired soldiers, the English will hop on board and finish them off.

The English can field a strong team – about 130 ships, but only 60 or so are fit to fight. The Spanish galleons are about 50 metres long, but the English ones are about half that length. As a result the English ships are much quicker. They have two other advantages; firstly, they pack some of the most accurate long range guns ever built, and secondly, most of them use the same standard size cannonball. Spanish ships have guns of different sizes and types, and finding the right size of cannonball for each gun during the heat of battle must be tricky!

! WISE UP WORDS

armada   galleon   muskets

Weapons file

- Spanish guns – These two-wheeled guns were difficult to move and aim. The Spanish preferred to get close and jump on board the enemy ships.

- English guns – These big, bronze blasters could fire heavy cannonballs from 150m away.

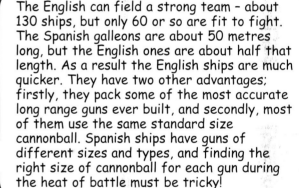

WORK

1 a Why did Philip decide to attack England in 1588?

   b What was his plan if his invasion was a success?

2 a In your own words, describe how an English or a Spanish ship's captain would try to defeat an enemy. You might wish to illustrate your answer.

   b In your opinion, which fleet of ships, the English or the Spanish, stood the best chance of success? Explain your answer carefully.

'God blew and they were scattered'

AIMS
▶ What went wrong for the Spanish Armada?
▶ Was the defeat of Spain a real turning point in the history of Europe?

King Philip's plan was an ambitious one. His fleet of 170 ships would sail up the English Channel to Calais and pick up Spanish soldiers waiting there for them. The force of 30 000 soldiers and sailors would cross the Channel, capture London and replace Queen Elizabeth with a Catholic monarch.

The Armada left Spain on 2 July 1588. They were immediately spotted by a fast sailing boat heading for England. News that the Spanish were on their way would reach England long before they arrived – the English would know they were coming.

6 The Spaniards flee. A sudden storm batters their ships as they struggle home around Scotland and Ireland.

5 Frightened by the fireships, the Spanish scatter in ones and twos, all over the North Sea. The fast English ships attack again and again.

4 Sir Francis Drake attacks the Spanish ships with a weapon they fear the most – FIRESHIPS. Eight old ships are filled with straw, gunpowder, tar and barrels of pig fat and then set alight. They act like floating bombs and drift towards the Spanish who panic when they see them.

3 The Spanish arrive in Calais on 5 August. They wait for soldiers to join them, but the soldiers do not arrive!

7 Nearly every Spanish ship is damaged. The sailors starve as their food goes mouldy. Injured men die when their wounds become infected. As ships sink, some sailors manage to stagger ashore, only to be attacked by the Scottish and Irish.

2 The Spanish are spotted off Cornwall on 29 July and **beacons** are lit on hilltops to warn people of a possible invasion. The English Navy chases the Spaniards for over one week but cannot sink a single Spanish ship.

1 170 ships set out, sailing packed together in a **crescent** shape, which the English would find difficult to attack.

8 Final Score
Spain:
2 ships captured
3 wrecked off France
2 wrecked off Holland
2 sunk in battle
19 wrecked off Scotland and Ireland
35 ships vanish, never to be seen again
England:
No English ships are lost
Thousands of sailors die of sickness and starvation
Surviving sailors don't even get paid when they return home

Task 3

Fill in the missing consonants to find the words. There are clues to help you.

_ _ i _ _ e _ _   E _ i _ a _ e _ _
Her father was absent at her christening

_ a _ _ _   _ u _ _ _
Famous animal

_ i _ _ i a _   _ _ a _ o _ _ o a _ e
Inventor of new words

_ a _ e _   _ u _ _ a _ e
Theatre builder

_ i _ _   _ _ i _ i _   o _   _ _ a i _
Tried to teach the English a lesson

_ i _   _ _ a _ _ i _   _ _ a _ e
Famous sea dog

_ a _ _ , _ u e e _   o _   _ _ o _ _
Was her second husband murdered by her next husband?

A _ _ _ o _ _   _ a _ i _ _ o _
Hatched a secret plan to kill Queen Elizabeth

_ o _ _   _ a _ i _ _
Slaving away

Task 4

Henry VII • James I • Elizabeth I • Henry VIII
• Edward VI • Mary I

a These are some of the monarchs you have met so far. Place them in the correct chronological order.

b Add the dates in which they ruled.

c Then add five brief facts about each king or queen. Make sure you write no more than ten words for each fact.

Task 5

The following sentences have no capital letters, commas or full stops. Copy them out correctly. Then underline the facts in blue and the opinions in red.

a king henry desperately wanted a son who could be king after him he must have hated his two daughters mary and elizabeth

b tudor schools were very strict you could be beaten for being late swearing gambling and forgetting books

c strolling players were groups of actors who travelled from village to village they were often joined by jugglers musicians and puppeteers

d despite queen elizabeth's attempts to keep her youthful looks she failed miserably she wore a wig because she was bald and had a mouthful of black teeth she was an ugly woman

e tudor women were probably all crazy to put harmful chemicals like sublimate of mercury on their faces it caused women's faces to flake like paint

f king philip of spain hated sir francis drake more than anyone else

g by 1568 elizabeth had been queen for ten years she hadn't married and she hadn't any children

h john hawkins was a cruel man who was responsible for shipping people as slaves to america

Task 6

The following words are anagrams – words with their letters jumbled up. See if you can put the letters in the correct order to spell a word. Use the clues to help you.

a SCUCSESRO James I was Elizabeth I's

b MPIOTRRES Men who brought goods like perfume into the country from other places in the world

c RATENOS A criminal act against your country

d PSNASIH MARDAA They thought they were 'invincible' against the English

e CISK PPUEARS These poor people were looked after in special homes

f HET LGBOE Shakespeare's place of work

g TEH LACPEPRDDGOEUN Wanted people to feel sorry for him

h CCHOU A HHAEGOSD Canting for 'sleep'

The Gunpowder Plot of 1605

▶ Why do we 'Remember, remember, the fifth of November'?
▶ Why is it difficult to get a clear picture of events in history?

The Gunpowder Plot of 1605 has all the ingredients of a brilliant crime story. A plan to kill the King, gunpowder, betrayal, prison, torture, gun battles, hanging and fireworks. What a story!

Most of you will know the story quite well. Your friends and family will probably know the same tale. But do you know the full story? Was Guy Fawkes 'set up'? Did King James know about the assassination plot all along?

These pages outline the familiar story of the Gunpowder Plot. The following pages then look at the evidence in detail. You'll have to make up your own mind – were Guy Fawkes and his Catholic plotters framed?

King James I

In 1605, there were laws passed against people who were Catholic. King James had even ordered Catholic priests to leave England or face execution. A small group of Catholics decided that they wanted James dead. They hoped a new king or queen would treat them better.

The Plot

Every year the king or queen officially opened Parliament. In 1605, Parliament was due to be opened on 5 November. Most of the powerful people in the country would go to watch – the ceremony still happens today. The plot was to blow up the King when he was in Parliament, seize his young daughter, Elizabeth, who lived in the Midlands and place her on the throne instead of James. Obviously, she would need help from elder people, who would be Catholic of course.

The Plotters

Their leader was the brave and handsome Robert Catesby. He was a devout Catholic who had gambled away much of his family's wealth. He was joined by Tom and Robert Winter, the Wright brothers (Chris and John), Thomas Percy and of course Guido – or Guy – Fawkes. Guy was an experienced soldier who was used to handling explosives. He would be responsible for lighting the gunpowder to be placed under Parliament. There were also many others who knew of the plan too.

Source A ▾ A picture of the plotters. It is unlikely that the artist ever saw the men.

Bates • Robert Winter • Christopher Wright • John Wright • Thomas Percy • Guido Fawkes • Robert Catesby • Tho Wint

Plan A: Early in 1604, Thomas Percy rented a house next to Parliament. The gang tried to tunnel under Parliament, just below where the King would sit. However, the tunnel soon filled with water.

Plan B: In spring 1605, Percy rented a cellar directly under Parliament. Thirty-six barrels of gunpowder were smuggled in and stored behind the piles of wood.

FAILED

What went wrong?

On 26 October 1605, a mysterious letter arrived at the house of a man called Lord Monteagle. The note contained a warning.

'I warn you … To devise some excuse to shift your attendance at the Parliament … they shall receive a terrible blow this Parliament and yet they shall not see who hurts them …'

Monteagle immediately took the note to Robert Cecil, who was the King's chief advisor. Cecil took the letter to the King.

Just after midnight on 5 November, the cellars below Parliament were searched. A tall, brown-haired man was found hanging around. He was holding a lantern and had with him a watch, matches and a tinderbox in his pockets. He said his name was John Johnson and that he worked for Thomas Percy. He was brought before King James but refused to answer any of his questions. The King then ordered that he be taken to the Tower of London and questioned. After two days of torture on the rack he gave his real name as Guido Fawkes. After another two days he told his torturers that he was there to blow up Parliament. After another six days, he named the other plotters.

What about the others?

When the other plotters realised the plan hadn't worked, they barricaded themselves in Holbeach House, near Dudley in the Midlands. They tried to dry out some of their wet gunpowder near a fire and, not surprisingly, it blew up. The noise from the explosion alerted the King's troops, who were searching nearby. After a shoot-out in which both Catesby and Percy were killed by the same bullet, the surviving plotters were arrested and taken to London. However, some would say Catesby and Percy were the lucky ones…

The Punishment

After a quick trial, the survivors, including Guy Fawkes, were sentenced to death. They were dragged through the streets of London, hung until they were nearly dead, cut down, cut open and their insides were pulled out and burned on a fire in front of them. Then their corpses were cut into pieces and put on display around the country.

FACT: ▶ Clever Guy!

▶ Guy Fawkes was probably dead before his punishment properly began. As he climbed up the scaffold steps with the hangman's noose around his neck, he jumped off, head first and broke his neck. The execution carried on regardless.

Source B ▲ A terrible punishment for the plotters

WORK

1 Explain what the plotters hoped to achieve by blowing up King James.

2 Write down the names of all the people involved in the Gunpowder Plot. Next to each one write down the role they played, for example, Lord Monteagle – was sent the letter warning him of the plot to blow up Parliament.

3 a Read the passage taken from the unsigned letter to Lord Monteagle.

   b In your own words, explain the meaning of the letter.

4 Why do you think King James ordered such a nasty execution for the plotters?

5 Imagine you were in London to witness the execution of Guy Fawkes and the remaining Catholic plotters. Write a letter to a friend describing the events of that day. Remember, at the time most people were pleased that the plot had failed.

6 How do many people remember the Gunpowder Plot today?

Newsflash: Charlie for the chop!

 AIMS
▶ How did King Charles spend his last few hours alive?
▶ What happened in the aftermath of his death?

We all know that there weren't any televisions at this time. There were no six o'clock news programmes, no newsflashes and certainly no special live reports. However, if there were, the events of Tuesday 30 January 1649 might have been presented like this...

TV Presenter: We are very sorry to interrupt your Tuesday afternoon film but the news we have been expecting has just been confirmed. Charles Stuart, King of England, is dead. Shortly after 2:00pm, he was beheaded outside Whitehall Banqueting House, London. Over to Annette Ball, our live reporter at the scene.

Live Reporter: Thank you Fiona, amazing scenes here in London today. The execution was planned for around 12 noon, so early this morning the King went for a walk through St James' Park with his pet spaniel Rogue. He ate some bread, drank some red wine and then insisted on putting on two shirts before he started his final journey.

TV Presenter: Why two shirts Annette?

Live Reporter: It's very chilly here today in London Fiona, and apparently Charles didn't want to start shivering from the cold. He didn't want the public to think that he was trembling with fear.

TV Presenter: You say that they planned to execute him at 12 noon but he was killed shortly after 2:00pm. Why the delay?

Live Reporter: Firstly, the usual executioner refused to do it. Then 38 other men were each offered £100 to do it. One by one they refused. Eventually, two men agreed to do it in disguise. They wore masks, wigs and false beards.

TV Presenter: So what happened next?

Live Reporter: The King arrived shortly before 2:00pm. He stepped out onto the black cloth-covered scaffold, took off his jewels and his cloak, and then tucked his hair into a cap. He spoke calmly to those men near to him, knelt down to pray and then put his head on the block.

TV Presenter: Was it a clean cut Annette?

Live Reporter: Yes it was Fiona. One clean chop. Then one of the axemen held up his head for all to see. One eyewitness told me, 'There was such a groan by the thousands then present, as I never heard before and desire I may never hear again.'

TV Presenter: Describe the scene now Annette.

Live Reporter: The King has just been taken away in a wooden coffin. Now people are paying to dip their handkerchiefs in the King's blood. Others are trying to break off pieces of the scaffold covered in his blood. Some of the soldiers guarding the scaffold will make a fortune today! Incredible scenes Fiona. What can the country expect next? Back to you in the studio...'

TV Presenter: That's the big question tonight. King Charles is dead... so what happens now? What will Parliament do?

That must have been the question on everyone's lips. With no king, what sort of job would Parliament do?

Source B ◄
A painting of
the execution,
painted soon
after the event

Source A ▼ A picture of the execution, made straight after the event

FACT: ▶ Did you know?

- The identity of the executioners is still a mystery.
- The execution block was 45cm long and 15cm wide. There was also special equipment to harness the King if he refused to put his head on the block.
- The King's head was sewn back on and he was quietly buried in Windsor Castle. In 1813, a doctor stole one of the King's neck bones and used it to hold salt at dinner parties. Queen Victoria wasn't amused and ordered him to put it back.

WISE UP WORD

bias

WORK

1. a Why do you think so many people refused to execute Charles? Give as many reasons as you can.

   b Why did the two men finally agree to do it?

   c Think carefully. Why did the executioners insist that Charles tuck his long hair into a cap?

2. Look at **Source A**. What is wrong with this print? Your answer to 1b might give you a clue.

3. a Look at **Source B**. You will notice four smaller pictures surrounding the main one. Describe what you think each of the smaller pictures shows.

   b Why do you think that the woman in the main picture has fainted?

   c Why do you think some people wanted to dip their handkerchiefs in the dead King's blood?

4. Many people didn't want Charles to die. Look back over pages 86 to 89 and write down as many examples as you can to show this.

5. Design a front page for a newspaper reporting the amazing events of Tuesday 30 January 1649. Try to do the following:

   - Write a version that favours the supporters of the King, or those who decided to execute him.

   - Show your report to a classmate and see if he or she can spot the parts of writing that show **bias**.

Whatever happened to Cromwell's head?

AIMS
▸ What happened in England after Cromwell's death?
▸ What happened to Cromwell's head after his death?

Oliver Cromwell, Lord Protector, died of **malaria** in September 1658. John Evelyn wrote in his diary 'November 22nd 1658: It was the joyfulest funeral I have ever saw, for there was none that cried but the dogs, which the soldiers hooted away with a barbarous nasty noise, drinking and taking tobacco on the streets as they went…'

PAUSE FOR THOUGHT

Sounds a bit strange doesn't it? A 'joyful funeral' where no one cries! It seems that many people weren't too upset at Cromwell's funeral – why? How did some of the soldiers show their attitude towards Cromwell?

Cromwell was buried at Westminster Abbey and his son, Richard, was made Lord Protector. He didn't really want the job and would sooner have been left alone as a farmer. Unable to stop the arguing between Parliament and the army, Richard resigned after only a few months. After a few more months of confusion, a new Parliament asked Charles I's son to return from exile abroad to become King. By 1660, the republic was over and England and Wales got a new King. One of King Charles II's first actions was a brutal one – kill the men who killed his father.

PAUSE FOR THOUGHT

How many men signed Charles I's death warrant (you might have to look back a few pages)? In signing away King Charles' life, many had signed away their own!

Fifteen of the men who had signed Charles I's death warrant were already dead by 1660, including Cromwell and Judge Bradshaw. The King ordered their bodies to be dug up and hung from the **gallows** at Tyburn. Some others had escaped abroad to America, several were arrested but died in prison, but thirteen of the **regicides** (king killers) were executed.

> **! WISE UP WORDS**
> malaria   gallows   regicide

So what about Cromwell's head?

WARNING: IT'S A VERY DISGUSTING TALE

1: 1658

Cromwell dies

Doctor Bates cuts out and weighs his brain. He says it weighs 82.5 ounces. The average brain weighs 49 ounces – Bates was probably lying. Why?

2: 1660

New King Charles II wants to punish Cromwell

Body dug up and hanged at Tyburn. His head was stuck on a pole outside Westminster Abbey.

2 YEARS AFTER DEATH

3: 1685

Head stays on pole for 24 years

Strong wind blows head off pole. It is found by a soldier called Barnes who takes it home and hides it in his chimney.

4: 1702

Barnes dies

He tells his family where he has hidden the head. They sell it to a Frenchman who puts it in a museum.

CROMWELL'S HEAD 1658

5: 1738

Museum owner dies

A young actor called Samuel Russell buys it. He pays his rent by charging people to see it.

One penny for a look

6: 1789

Russell sells head

A group of businessmen buy the head for £230. It goes on display in Bond Street, London.

£230

7: 1814

Dr Wilkinson buys head

He keeps the head in a box, wrapped in silk. He writes that an ear is missing, there's a hole in the top where a pole has been and there are axe marks on the neck.

DEFECTS

8: 1935

Doctor examines the head

They decide that the man has definitely had his head cut off and that the pimples and warts *do* match Cromwell's portrait.

9: 1960

Wilkinson's family gives head away

The head is given to Cromwell's old college, Sidney Sussex, in Cambridge. The head was buried secretly. It is still there today.

Cromwell's head buried near here

Source A ▶ Oliver Cromwell, painted in 1650. He told the artist, 'Do not flatter me at all, but show all the wrinkles, pimples and warts.'

Source B ▾ A photo of the remains of Cromwell's head. You were told it was a disgusting tale!

WORK

1 a What does the word 'regicide' mean?

  b Why do you think Charles II wanted to punish all the men involved in his father's death – even the ones who were already dead?

2 Read the story of Cromwell's head carefully.

  a Why do you think soldier Barnes hid the head?

  b Why do you think Dr Wilkinson was convinced that he had bought Cromwell's head?

  c What evidence did the doctors have in 1935 that the head was Cromwell's?

  d Why do you think the head was finally buried in secret?

  e Today, experts know where Cromwell's head is buried but can they ever *really* be sure that it is actually Cromwell's head? Think carefully about your answer.

3 Prepare and act out a short role-play called 'The story of Cromwell's head':

  • Write out a script

  • Take on some of the roles in the story, for example, Bates, Barnes, Russell

  • Find a suitable 'head' (an old football perhaps)

  • Act it out in class

A new London is built

 AIMS

‣ How was London rebuilt?
‣ What were Christopher Wren's plans for a new London?

Before the Great Fire, London was for the most part a filthy stinking maze of streets and alleys full of dirt and disease. Fire destroyed five-sixths of the city and planning for the rebuilding of it began soon after the fire was finally out.

The King asked for plans for a new city and within two weeks an **architect** called Christopher Wren had written up his ideas. He planned a city with broad, straight streets, wide-open spaces and magnificent new brick or stone churches and homes.

Despite Wren's ideas for a magnificent new city, most of them were ignored. Homeless people wanted their homes built quickly and in exactly the same places as their old ones. Few people wanted to – or could afford to – give up their land to make London a nicer place to live. However, the King insisted on some changes.

PAUSE FOR THOUGHT

> Why do you think Wren's plans for a new London included **BROAD** streets, **WIDE**-open spaces and **BRICK** or **STONE** buildings?

Source A ▾ A map of London made soon after the fire. The white area is the part that was destroyed by fire. Look for i) the plans for a new London
  ii) a picture of the fire

New regulations for New London

- Building new homes out of wood is *BANNED*
- All new houses should be built of *BRICK* or *STONE*
- All new streets must be *WIDE*
- Houses over nine metres wide are only allowed on main streets
- 100 existing streets must be *WIDENED*
- The filthy Fleet River will be covered over and some new common **sewers** will be built

Fire started here

Source B ▶ People would display a **fire mark** on the outside of their house to prove their insurance fees had been paid.

By 1672, a new city had risen from the ashes. London looked like it had been planned properly – rows of houses, all the same height, made from the same building materials. Cleaner streets meant fewer rats and fleas. Stone buildings meant less chance of fire. Never again was there a plague or fire on the same scale as the ones of 1665 and 1666.

One of Wren's ideas that everyone loved was his plan for 51 new churches. The most famous, St Paul's Cathedral, took 35 years to build. By the time he died in 1723, Wren had been asked to build other magnificent buildings, including colleges and hospitals. Wren is buried in St Paul's. If you visit his grave, you will find the words Si Monumentum Requiris Circumspice – they mean, 'If you seek his monument, look around you.'

FACT: ▶ New London, new ideas

▶ Insurance companies started up as a result of the Great Fire. Before, if your house burned down, you paid for it to be rebuilt. From 1666 onwards, a house owner could pay small sums of money to insure their property. If a fire started, the employees of the insurance company would put out the fire using their own fire engine.

! WISE UP WORDS

sewers   fire mark   architect

WORK

1 a How much of London was destroyed by the fire?

   b What sort of new city did Christopher Wren plan? Give reasons for his ideas.

   c Why were all his plans not used?

   d Do you think Wren's grave inscription is an appropriate one?

2 a Explain the phrase 'blessing in disguise'. You might like to discuss this with a classmate or your teacher.

   b How might the Great Fire of London be seen as a 'blessing in disguise'?

3 Write an essay to answer the following question: 'How and why did London change from 1660 to 1672?'

   Your essay should include:

   • A paragraph or two about London in 1660, including information on the streets, housing, health and hygiene.

   • A paragraph on the disasters to hit London in 1665 and 1666.

   • A conclusion about the changes to London in 1666 and the reasons for them.

9 • Medical advances

Getting better?

 AIMS
- ▸ Why were battlefields such dangerous places?
- ▸ How did Ambroise Paré change medical treatment forever?

One of the most dangerous and unpleasant places to be in Tudor or Stuart England was on the battlefield. A soldier faced death or wounding from cannonballs, bullets, swords, arrows, pikes, daggers and axes.

If the army you fought in had a doctor, he wouldn't care too much about hygiene or pain relief. His instruments may have been dropped in the mud a few times, and his old robes would be soaked in the blood of his previous patients. In these conditions, damaged limbs usually became infected. If you were unlucky enough to need a limb **amputated**, a blow on the head to knock you out would be the best pain relief you could hope for. Most badly injured soldiers died of shock, blood loss or infection.

But things were about to change. A young French army doctor called Ambroise Paré started to use different methods to treat wounds. He based a lot of his theories on the work of Andreas Vesalius, a professor of surgery at Padua Medical School, Italy. Vesalius cut up bodies to see how they worked and wrote one of the first scientific textbooks on the human body in 1543. Paré wrote his own book – Works on Surgery – in 1575, and changed medical treatment forever.

Source A ▾ A picture of a wounded soldier from a book dated 1536 on surgery. Can you list the different injuries on this soldier's body?

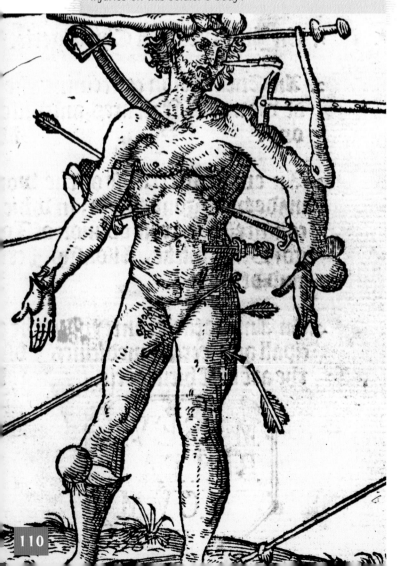

Old Treatment

- Pour boiling oil, mixed with cobwebs, onto gunshot wounds.
- Stop bleeding after amputation by putting a red-hot iron onto the wound.
- To rid the injured body of the 'poisons' of a gunshot wound, rub Egyptian mummy dust and powdered unicorn horn into the wound.

New Treatment

- Rub soothing ointment onto the wound and cover with clean bandages.
- Tie off the **artery** with a **ligature** to stop the blood flow.
- Don't try mummy dust or unicorn horn – it's absolutely useless! Try the ointment and bandages instead.

Paré even designed artificial limbs to replace amputated ones. His artificial arms had springs, pulleys, cogs and joints that made the elbow bend and the hand open and close.

Source B ▾ Paré's artificial limbs

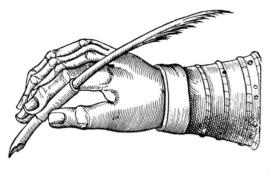

A scientific approach

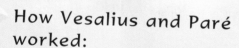

How Vesalius and Paré worked:

1 Observe what happens

2 Develop a theory

3 Use an experiment to test the theory

4 Observe and measure the results of the experiment

5 If the results aren't what you expect, revise the theory

You should recognise this approach to problems from your science lessons. The work of Vesalius and Paré inspired other scientists to ask questions, try their own experiments and find out about the world they lived in. Their work would inspire a new scientific age.

 FACT: ▶ A Royal supporter

▶ Charles II greatly admired the work of scientists. In 1662, he allowed a group of them to call themselves the 'Royal Society'. They met each week to discuss their experiments and ideas. Members still meet today. Prince Rupert was a member and even allowed scientists to cut open his skull, take out some of his brain cells and study them.

① WISE UP WORDS

ligature   amputated   artery

WORK

1 What other dangers faced a wounded soldier *after* he had been injured?

2 Look at **Source A**.

 a Draw your own version of the injured soldier.

 b List the different injuries on the soldier's body.

 c Why do you think the artist drew the picture?

3 a Do you think Paré improved a soldier's chances of surviving a nasty wound? Explain your answer carefully.

 b What was important about the way Paré and Vesalius worked?

4 a How did the Royal Society help the increase in new scientific ideas?

 b How did the printing press help the spread of ideas?

HUNGRY FOR MORE?

Some brilliant scientists lived between 1485 and 1750. Their discoveries formed the basis of much of the knowledge we have about the world today. In small groups, choose a famous scientist from this list and prepare a fact file on him or her. Share your findings with the group and prepare a class presentation called 'Famous scientists and their discoveries 1485–1750'.

Nicholas Copernicus – mathematics and astronomy

Edmund Halley – astronomy

William Harvey – circulation of the blood

Antony van Leeuwenhoek – the microscope

Robert Boyle – chemistry

Sir Isaac Newton – mathematics, light and gravity

Lady Mary Wortley – disease research

Can you cure King Charles II?

▶ Could you have been an effective Stuart doctor?
▶ What treatments were used on Charles II in 1685?

In Stuart times, approaches to medicine were a combination of different ideas. Some were very clever... but others were just crazy! Some doctors were beginning to work out exactly how the human body worked. Others hadn't got a clue! One of the most widely used cures was '**bloodletting**'. This was based on an old Greek and Roman idea that too much blood in a person's body was the cause of their illness. The answer was to cut the patient and let out the 'bad blood'. Soon their body would be back 'in balance' again. Needless to say, it didn't work, but it didn't stop some of England's most famous doctors from trying it.

The King is ill

What to do

1 Read each of the 'How's he feeling?' boxes carefully. They will give you some idea of the King's condition.

2 Choose a treatment from the list. You have to have a good reason to make your choice.

3 Record your choice and make a note of the reason.

Best of Luck!

How's he feeling? 2 February

After collapsing, the King has been unconscious for two hours. As the doctors arrive, he begins to wake up. He is in pain.

At 8:00am on 2 February 1685, Charles II fainted. It was soon clear that he was very ill. A dozen doctors gathered around his body. This was their chance to prove themselves as great doctors. If they could save him they would be richly rewarded. Fail and the King dies, and nobody wanted the blame for that!

Like all doctors, they had a choice of treatments. Imagine that you were one of the King's doctors. You will be given a series of choices to make based on real treatments available at the time. Can you cure King Charles II?

Treatment 1   What do you do?

Do you:

a Open up a vein in his arm and drain 16 ounces of blood, then make him vomit?

b Do nothing and wait to see if he gets any better?

c Wash his hair in urine?

He's just as bad. You must keep trying.

Treatment 2 What will you do next?

Do you:

a Bleed him again, perhaps 8 ounces of blood from his shoulder this time?

b Shave his head and burn his scalp to make it blister?

c Pray?!

How's he feeling? 3 February

The King is speaking again but still feels poorly. He still faints occasionally but recovers sooner than the day before.

Treatment 3 What do you do?

Do you:

a Suggest injecting him with antibiotics?

b Drain more blood and then pump a liquid up his bottom to make him empty his bowels!?

c Leave him alone, he seems better today – perhaps he is getting well?

How's he feeling? 4 February

He wakes up bright and early but collapses again at dinner time. He seems to be getting worse.

Treatment 4 What do you do?

Do you:

a Bleed him again – more than before today?

b Give him powdered human skull in a sweet drink – this is viewed by many as a super cure for any illness?

c Call another doctor; perhaps he can help more than you. Some people are saying that herbal remedies can work really well?

How did Britain change from 1485 to 1750?

AIMS ▸ What important ideas and inventions appeared between 1485 and 1750?

This book covers the years 1485 to 1750. During this time, some amazing and lasting changes took place. New ideas and discoveries altered the way people looked at the world, whilst new inventions changed the way people did things. Read this section carefully. It doesn't feature all the changes, discoveries and inventions that took place between 1485 and 1750, but it tries to pick out some of the most important and interesting ones.

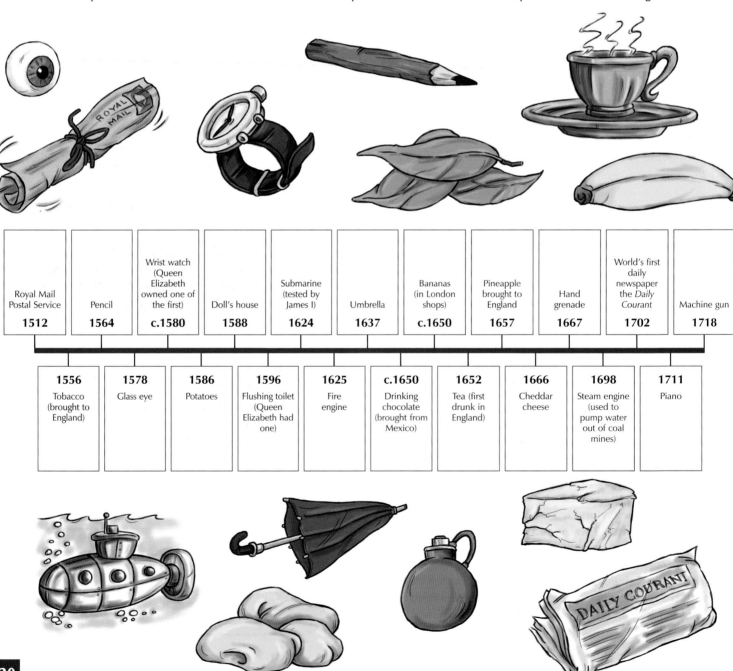

| Royal Mail Postal Service 1512 | Pencil 1564 | Wrist watch (Queen Elizabeth owned one of the first) c.1580 | Doll's house 1588 | Submarine (tested by James I) 1624 | Umbrella 1637 | Bananas (in London shops) c.1650 | Pineapple brought to England 1657 | Hand grenade 1667 | World's first daily newspaper the *Daily Courant* 1702 | Machine gun 1718 |

| 1556 Tobacco (brought to England) | 1578 Glass eye | 1586 Potatoes | 1596 Flushing toilet (Queen Elizabeth had one) | 1625 Fire engine | c.1650 Drinking chocolate (brought from Mexico) | 1652 Tea (first drunk in England) | 1666 Cheddar cheese | 1698 Steam engine (used to pump water out of coal mines) | 1711 Piano |

1485	1750
King in control	Parliament has more power than ever before
Disunited Kingdom	United Kingdom
Two kings (one in England, one in Scotland), different Parliaments	One king, one Parliament
Many explorers, but none know the continent of America exists 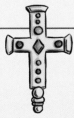	Continent of America discovered in 1492. Britain trades more and more with the newly discovered lands
Population	
England 2.25m, Wales 0.2m, Scotland 0.5m, Ireland 0.8m	England and Wales 6.25m, Scotland 1.25m, Ireland 3.25m, British settlers overseas 3.0m
3.75 million	**13.75 million** (including three million living abroad)
Religion	
Everyone Catholic 	Most members of Church of England (Protestant), some still Catholic
Medicine	
Very little known about science and the human body	Many new ideas

FACT: ▶ Sweet stuff

▶ Sir Francis Drake was the first Englishman to sail around the world. When he got back, he described one of the 'new' things he had seen. Can you guess what he is describing?

'This plant was as big as a human head. The back is full of string but if you take it off you come to a hard shell which is full of sweet liquid. Inside the shell is a hard, white substance as sweet as almonds and half an inch thick.'

WORK

1 a Inventions and new ideas change things. Choose five of the inventions or new ideas. Write how you think each may have helped to change things.

   b Are there any inventions you can see that you think have had little effect on our lives? Think carefully about your answer.

2 Using these pages and the work you have completed throughout this book, answer the following question. Your teacher will help you plan your essay answer.

'How was the Britain of 1485 different to the Britain of 1750?'

3 The 'Daily Courant' was the world's first daily newspaper. It started in 1702. Produce your own newspaper reporting for the period 1485–1750. Write articles for each of the following headlines:

Church News
Heroes
Women's Page
Crimes and Punishments
Sport and Entertainment Section
Problem Page
Death, Health and Medicine

Give your newspaper a suitable name. Perhaps you could work as a group and divide the work between you.

A United Kingdom?

▶ How did England gain control of Ireland, Wales and Scotland?

▶ By 1750, how united was the United Kingdom?

In 1485, England, Scotland and Ireland were separate countries. Wales was mostly controlled by the English, but parts of it were still ruled by the Welsh. Britain was <u>not</u> united. By 1750, Britain was a United Kingdom – how did this change take place?

Wales

In 1284, King Edward I of England said that Wales was under his control. In reality, he only controlled some of it. The rest was run by Welsh princes. It continued like this for over 250 years. Then in 1536, Henry VIII made all of Wales part of England. It was called the 'Act of Union'. English law replaced Welsh law and Welsh officials were forced to learn English.

Wales was even divided into 13 counties, and later each sent an MP to Parliament in London. Despite this, many Welsh traditions survived, including the Welsh language. By 1750, there may have been more people living in London than there were in all of Wales, but the Welsh language and many other customs continued to be used and passed on to future generations.

Ireland

English kings and queens had always tried to control Ireland. Brutal English armies had invaded many times but the Irish remained determined to keep the English out. They failed. Under King William III (Mary II's husband), the English finally defeated the Irish army in 1691. English Protestants – although making up only 25% of the population – owned 97% of the land. The rich landowning Protestants introduced new laws:

The deep divisions caused by England's actions in Ireland would not be repaired for many years, and some might say we still see the consequences today.

Irish Catholics CANNOT:

• Be lawyers, teachers or soldiers
• Own horses worth over £5
• Hold a government job
• Wear a sword
• Be a Member of Parliament or vote in elections

By Order of the English Parliament

Scotland

From 1603, the English and the Scots had shared the same monarch but had separate Parliaments, religions, laws and education systems.

Financially, Scotland was much poorer than England but was always friendly with England's arch-enemy, France. England found this threatening but neither Scotland nor England wanted war. Instead, the two countries decided to officially join together with the Act of Union in 1707. The Scottish Parliament was closed and they sent their MPs to London instead. The Scots kept their own laws, religions and school systems.

Queen Anne was the first monarch to call herself Queen of Great Britain and Ireland after the Act of Union with Scotland on 1 May 1707. This didn't mean that the Irish, Welsh and Scottish were happy with this situation. Far from it. When Queen Anne died in 1714, her distant relative, George I, became King. During his reign, there were several rebellions against English rule. In Scotland, there were rebellions in 1715 and 1745: both were crushed by the English. By 1750, it seemed that England, Scotland, Ireland and Wales were united, but not everyone was pleased about it.

FACT: ▶ Bonnie Prince Charlie

▶ Some Scots still wanted the **descendants** of James II to be their king. These people were called **Jacobites**. Jacobite comes from the Latin word for James.

In Scotland in 1745, a rebellion against English rule was led by James II's grandson, Charles Edward Stuart. He was better known as Bonnie Prince Charlie. He won control of Scotland and then invaded England. He thought some Englishmen might join his army but none did so. He was forced to march back to Scotland. At Culloden, the English army caught up with him and defeated his forces. Charlie escaped to France dressed as a woman!

The Battle of Culloden was the last battle fought on British soil.

Source A ▼ A 'Wanted' poster for Bonnie Prince Charlie

WISE UP WORDS

Jacobite   descendants

WORK

1   In your books, construct a timeline covering the years 1485–1750. The title for your timeline should read: 'How united was the United Kingdom?' Mark the following dates onto your timeline, including a few sentences explaining the importance of each:

1536 • 1603 • 1691 • 1707 • 1714 • 1715 • 1745

2   Which nation seems to be the force behind uniting Britain? Explain your answer.

3   What methods were used to ensure Wales, Ireland and Scotland came under the control of the English crown?

4   What advantages do you think English monarchs during the period 1485–1750 saw in having England, Wales, Ireland and Scotland as a United Kingdom?

Have you been learning?

Task 1

a Look at **Source A** carefully. Make a list of all the different activities you can see. Here are two to start you off. 1: Archery 2: A man selling knives and combs

b The City of London is in the background. Find two famous London landmarks and write a sentence about each of them.

Source A ▾ People enjoying themselves at the London Frost Fair of 1684. It took place whenever the River Thames froze solid in winter.

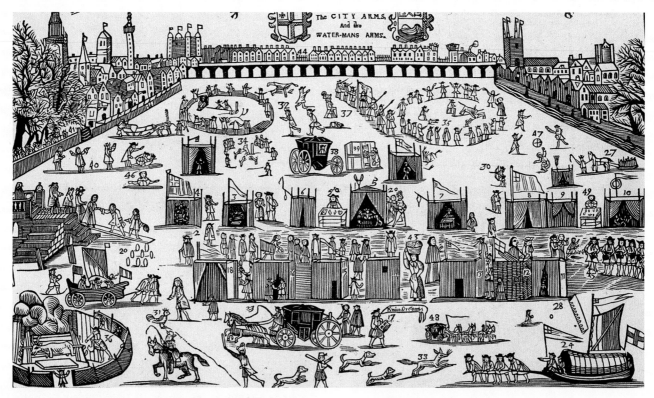

Task 2

Design a poster for the London Frost Fair of 1684. Remember to include:

• Where and when

• Details of displays, entertainment and attractions

• Information about who will be attending (see **Source B**)

• A picture designed to attract fun-seekers

Source B ▴ A souvenir printed ticket for the fair. You could pay to have your name put alongside the special royal guests.

Task 3

Below are 12 sentences about the traditional story of the Gunpowder Plot – some of them are true and some are false. Correct the false ones and then place them all in the correct chronological order.

a   The gang tried to tunnel under Parliament where the Queen was to sit.

b   Lady Monteagle received a warning letter about a plot to kill the King.

c   Thomas Casey rented a house next to Parliament.

d   The cellars below Buckingham Palace were searched and a man by the name of John Johnson was found there. He was taken to the King.

e   The tunnel plan failed when it filled with custard.

f   The noise from the exploding gunpowder alerted the King's troops. After a shoot-out, killing Catesby and Percy, the remaining plotters were arrested.

g   Percy then rented a cellar under Parliament. He smuggled in barrels of gunpowder and hid them behind piles of wood.

h   The letter was taken to Robert Redford, the King's chief advisor, and then to the King.

i   After a quick trial, the plotters along with Guy Fawkes were set free.

j   John Johnson refused to answer the King's questions. He was taken to McDonald's and after 20 days of torture there, he revealed his real name – Guido Fawkes.

k   The remaining plotters, aware that the plan had failed, barricaded themselves into Holbeach House in the Midlands.

Task 4

Below are five groups of words. Work out which is the odd one out in each and say why.

a   Tom Winter • Chris Wright • Guy Fawkes
    • Robert Winter • Tom Percy

b   Parliamentarians • Roundheads • Royalists
    • New Model Army

c   Edgehill • Naseby • Bosworth • Marston Moor

d   Playing football • Praying in church
    • Dancing and singing • Drinking beer

e   fleas • boils • fever • rash • sneezing

Task 5

Imagine that you are watching a video film of the events in history you have been studying. Someone has pressed 'pause' and frozen the picture. In groups, pretend that you are characters from history captured in the 'freeze frame'. When you have worked with your group to produce a freeze frame, why not show the remainder of your class and see if they can guess the event that you have chosen.

Here are some events that you could 'freeze':

• The execution of Guy Fawkes
• The Great Plague
• The execution of King Charles
• The Great Fire of London

Task 6

The first daily newspaper didn't appear in England until 1702. Before then, information travelled by word of mouth, expensive printed books or by broadsheet – a large, single sheet of paper containing details of major events.

Try to imagine that there were daily newspapers throughout Tudor and Stuart times. Here are a few headlines you might have seen:

• **1537: EDDIE'S HERE!**
• **1588: THE BIGGER THEY COME, THE ARMADA THEY FALL**
• **1605: FAWKES FAILS**
• **1649: CROMWELL'S CREW CHOP CHARLIE**
• **1665: IT'S BACK!**
• **1666: INFERNO**

a   Write a sentence or two explaining each headline.

b   In small groups, write a newspaper article about each of the headlines. You could add some of your own headlines and stories. Your work could make an interesting class display.

Glossary

Acre   A measure of land, roughly equivalent to just over half a football pitch.

Adulterous   An adulterous person is a married man or woman who is not faithful to their wife or husband.

Allies   Two groups on the same side. Friends in battle.

Amputate   To cut off a leg, arm, hand, finger or toe.

Antibiotics   A chemical substance used to destroy bacteria.

Architect   A designer of buildings.

Armada   A fleet of warships.

Artery   One of the tubes carrying blood from the heart.

Beacon   A fire, used to give a warning signal.

Belladonna   A chemical used by Tudor women to make their eyes shine and sparkle.

Bias   Showing favouritism for one side or the other. Something that is 'biased' is one-sided.

Bill of Mortality   A weekly list of the causes of death in a particular place.

Birch   A bundle of twigs tied together and used to hit children as a punishment. A cane was a single piece of wood.

Bloodletting   The practice of making someone bleed to cure an illness.

Blood sports   Sports that involve cruelty to animals.

Bubonic   One type of plague, named after one of its symptoms – buboes or boils.

Canting   A secretive street language used by sturdy beggars.

Catholic   A follower of the Catholic religion, one of the main Christian religions.

Cavaliers   Nickname for the King's soldiers during the English Civil War.

Cavalry   Soldiers on horseback.

Citizen   A person who lives in a town.

Civil war   A war between two groups of people in the same country.

Cobblestones   Large stones used to make roads and pathways.

Cochineal   A red dye or colouring, obtained from insects.

Colony   An area of land in a new country occupied by people who still remain under the rule of their homeland.

Contemporary   Something from the same period of time.

Continent   A very large area of land, such as Africa or Europe.

Crescent   A half-moon shape.

Cuckolding   Being a married man but having 'affairs' with married women was called cuckolding in Tudor England.

Cudgelling   A painful game involving hitting your opponent.

Death warrant   A piece of paper ordering someone's execution.

Descendants   Relatives.

Dissolution   The act of officially breaking up an organisation. It is the word used to describe the time when Henry VIII closed all the monasteries in England and Wales.

Divine right   The belief that kings and queens could do as they wished because they were appointed by God.

Ducking stool   A punishment for 'unruly' wives.

Embryo   An unborn baby in the early stages of development.

Enslavement   To make slaves of people.

Excommunicated   Expelled from the Catholic Church. A very serious religious punishment.

Execution   The process of killing or beheading an enemy or convicted criminal.

Explorer   A person who travels across land or sea to find new and undiscovered places.

Familiar   An animal, used by a witch to help her in her work.

Galleon   A large warship.

Gallery   A place to sit in a theatre.

Gallows   The framework upon which guilty criminals were hanged.

Genius   A person with great ability.

Gentlemen   Rich men, often dukes, earls or lords. They often own a lot of land.

Hornbook   A flat, double-sided paddle, shaped like a table-tennis bat. Used to help pupils read and write.

Imported   Brought in from another country, usually by boat.

Independent   Free from the control of another country.

Indulgences   You could 'buy' these from a bishop. They helped a person pass through purgatory quicker.

Infantry   Foot soldiers.

Inscription   Words written on a plaque, statue, monument or building.

Jacobite   A supporter of Catholic James II and his relatives, in particular 'Bonnie Prince Charlie'.

Justice of the Peace   A government official who tried to keep law and order in the towns.

Labourer   An ordinary working person, like a peasant of the Middle Ages.

Laxative   A medicine used to help a person go to the toilet easily.

Ligature   A tie, used to stop blood flow.

Lord Protector   Oliver Cromwell's title as ruler of England.

Major general   One of the eleven area leaders used by Oliver Cromwell to help him run England.

Malaria   A disease spread by mosquitoes.

Martyr   A person who dies because of what they believe.

Merchant   A person whose job is to buy and sell goods in order to make a profit.

Monarch   A king or queen. A country ruled by a king or queen is called a monarchy.

Musket   A gun.

Musketeer   A soldier who carries a musket.

Native Americans   The tribesmen who have lived on the continent of America for thousands of years. Sometimes incorrectly called 'Red Indians' or 'Redskins'.

Natives   Members of the original race of a country. They were born there and have not been brought there by people.

New Model Army   Parliament's highly trained professional army during the later stages of the English Civil War.

Offer of quarter   An opportunity for one side to surrender during a battle.

Origins   The start of something.

Parliamentarian   A supporter of Parliament during the English Civil War.

Pauper   Someone with no job. They rely on charity.

Perseverance   Trying hard over a long period of time.

Philosophy   The study of different theories about life.

Pike   A long pole, tipped with a steel spike. Used as a weapon.

Pikeman   A soldier who carries a pike.

Pilgrim Fathers   The name given to the first Puritan settlers in America in 1620.

Pit   The standing area nearest the stage in a theatre.

Playwright   A person who writes plays.

Pneumonia   A disease affecting the lungs.

Poor Law   A law that helped the poor by providing them with charity, such as food and shelter.

Pope   The leader of the Catholic Church, who lives in Rome.

Population   All the people who live in a particular place.

Precedent   A previous case or time something has happened that can be followed as an example.

Printing press   A machine used to print books.

Propaganda   False or misleading information used to spread a certain point of view.

Protestant   A person who protested against the beliefs of the Catholic Church. They believed in changing the ways in which God was worshipped.

Purgatory   The place between heaven and hell. A person was punished in purgatory for any sins they had committed on earth whilst alive.

Puritan   A strict Protestant who wanted to worship God very simply.

Quill pen   A pen made from feather. Dipped in ink to write.

Reformation   The name used to describe the changes or reforms made to the Catholic Church in the sixteenth century, mainly by Henry VIII and his son, later King Edward VI.

Regicide   The official word for killing a king or queen.

Renaissance   The period between the fourteenth and sixteenth centuries in Europe when there was a rebirth in art, literature and learning.

Republic   A country not ruled by a king or queen.

Revolution   To get rid of a country's leader or monarch by force.

Ridicule   To make fun of someone in an unkind way.

Roundheads   Nickname for Parliament's soldiers during the English Civil War.

Royalist   A supporter of the King during the English Civil War.

Sash   A coloured strip of cloth used to identify soldiers in battle.

Searchers   People who looked for dead bodies or plague victims during the Great Plague of 1665.

Sewer   A drain to remove waste water and sewage.

Shin-hacking   A painful game involving kicking your opponent.

Ship tax   A charge, introduced by Charles I, for people living by the sea.

Shorthand   A type of coded writing that can be written quickly.

Slave   A person owned by another and forced to do what the owner wants.

Sphere   Ball-shaped.

Spices   Strong-smelling powder or seeds from a plant added to food to give it flavour.

Spinster   An unmarried older woman.

Stillborn   A baby born dead.

Strolling players   A group of travelling actors, musicians and entertainers.

Sturdy beggars   Criminals who used clever tricks to get money.

Successor   Next in line to the throne.

Superstitious   A belief in omens and ghosts. For example, the fear of the number 13.

Symbol   Sign or thing that stands for something. For example, a cross is a symbol of the church.

Symptoms   Signs of illness or disease.

Torture   The use of special equipment that causes terrible pain in order to get a criminal to admit their guilt.

Treason   A crime against the king or queen.

Tuberculosis   A lung disease.

Voyage   A journey.

Wife sale   A type of divorce. In Tudor and Stuart England, it was possible to sell your wife at a 'wife sale'.

Witchcraft   The use of magic or spells by witches.

Yeoman   A farmer – some were rich; others were poor.

Yield   To give in or surrender.

Index

This Book
Belongs to

_____

For Erin Mae x – M. R.

For Joshua – T. McL.

Michelle Robinson & Tom McLaughlin

CHICKEN NUGGET

Burger
(My big brother)

Mama

Fillet

My name is Nugget,
Chicken Nugget.
This is my family.
I'm the smallest.

↑
& Drumstick
(the twins)

Being the smallest is a pain in the beak.
I have the smallest bedroom.

The smallest portions.

And only the tiniest bit
of space on the sofa.

I have to stand on my tiptoes just to reach the height chart.

I asked Mama to move it, but she didn't listen.

The same thing happened when
Burger told me to go in goal.

"But I'm scared,"
I said.

Did anybody listen? Nope.

When you're little, nobody ever does.

Then this morning my new, long-lost cousin, Franz, turned up. He's a funny-looking chicken – he's really tall and his feathers are kind of furry.

Everyone else went crazy over him.
Not me. I ran away and hid.

But I needn't have worried.
Franz turned out to be
surprisingly
friendly.

He fitted right in. And did he leave me
out because I was the smallest?
No way.

"We're family," he said.
"And families
STICK
together."

Henopoly

I really wanted Franz to come to
nursery with me, so I plucked up
the courage and asked him.

"How delightful," said Franz.
"I'd LOVE to eat –
I mean **meet** –
ALL of your friends."

Cool or what?

I bet nobody else had a cousin
like Franz. I was SO excited . . .

I'm normally shy at nursery, but Franz helped me come out of my shell.

At snack time, he ignored all the fruit and got **stuck into** the toys.

And when we went to play outside he made up the BEST game.

At home time, Miss Sweet-And-Sour
said Franz had quite an appetite.

"Oh, this is nothing," said Franz.
"I'll be cooking dinner at Nugget's
house tonight. A **proper** dinner.
You should come."

I was AMAZED.
We'd never had a teacher for dinner.
Franz even said I could help him cock!

But when we got home
everything changed.
I asked for a job to do,
but – as usual –
no one listened.

Not EVEN
Franz.

Easy Chicken Dishes

Nobody wanted me around, so I went
to my tiny room all by my tiny self.
It's not like anyone would notice
if I wasn't at dinner.

Although something
did smell good.

So I sneaked
downstairs
to grab a
bite to eat . . .

Once the police had taken Franz away, the TV people listened to *everything* I had to say.

Everyone else did, too.

Would you believe Franz wasn't my long-lost cousin after all?

CAUGHT!

Get this – he wasn't EVEN a chicken.

I know!

My name is Nugget
and this is my family.

Fillet & Drumstick
(the twins)

Burger
(My big brother)

Nugget
(that's me)

Mama

I'm the smallest –
but I don't mind.

national
Bravery
Awards

Sometimes even the **bravest** HERO . . .

...is just *a little* chicken!